# AMAZED BY SPAIN

## How an unexpected legacy changed our lives

SUSAN SHENTON

Text copyright ©2019 Susan Shenton

The author has asserted her moral right under the Copyright, Designs and Patents Act, 1988, to be identified as the author of this work.

All rights reserved. No part of this publication may be reproduced, stored in a retrieval system, or transmitted, in any form or by any means, without the prior permission in writing of the publisher.

# 1

"I guess it's becoming pretty normal now," my husband Paul said as he stood by the table, dressed in lycra and sweating profusely. He was fiddling with a digital gadget which he must have taken from the bike he'd just been riding in the garage.

"Did you hear what I said?" I asked, wondering if he was referring to his heart rate or other data essential to the middle-aged cycling buff.

"Yes. I mean, Brits have been living in Spain for so long now that quite a lot'll be popping their clogs and leaving houses in their wills."

"Yes, but Aunt Jean's left this particular one to me. Aren't you excited?"

He wiped his shiny forehead and shrugged. "I'd rather have had her savings. Will Linda get her savings?"

I sighed. "It's not as simple as that, but yes, it seems that my sister is the beneficiary of some of her more liquid assets, while I get the house."

He shrugged again and a drop of sweat fell from his chin. "Well, it'll be easy enough to flog it, I suppose. There are plenty of dumb sun worshippers who want to go and laze about out there. Where was it again?"

"It *is* in the mountains inland from the Alicante coast. I have many fond memories of the place."

"Hmm, distant memories."

"Yes, well, if she hadn't married that Spanish ogre we'd have carried on going."

"It's a bloody miracle you're still in her will, both of you."

I nodded slowly. "Hmm, still in it or, er… recently in it."

He grinned. "Yeah, those plane tickets might have been the best investment you ever made. I'll go and shower."

"Do."

I'd better explain. Our intrepid Aunt Jean moved to Spain in 1976, intent on pursuing her career as an artist and renouncing future matrimonial ties forever and ever. Her first marriage to an irascible dentist had ended in mutual loathing after thirteen years and no children, but she'd found herself financially in the pink and thoroughly fed up of our Staffordshire town, so she hopped it to Spain at the age of thirty-nine and bought a large house in a small village for next to nothing. I was just eighteen and my sister Linda twenty, so in the hot summer of '76 we jumped at the chance of going abroad for the first time, if you don't count a day trip to Calais, which we didn't.

The coach trip to Valencia was hell, but the slow train journey which followed was charming, its final miles passing through tunnels and wooded ravines en route to the large, sombre town of Alcoy, where Aunt Jean met us at the station in her light-blue Citroen Dyane. From there she drove us along increasingly rough roads eastwards into the hills to a small village, not as white as we'd imagined, but quaint all the same. She was the first foreigner to live there since the Moors had been driven out in the thirteenth century – or so a droll teacher from a neighbouring village told her

– and despite her rudimentary Spanish the locals had embraced her as an exotic curiosity.

One day I might try to write about the three summer trips we made to see Aunt Jean during the following five years, but this account is about modern times, so I'll just mention the last trip, when a big man called Juan had somehow wheedled his way into her life. Linda and I soon christened him the Ogre, as he was an old, ugly, uncouth local farmer whose charms we simply couldn't see. He resented us taking up his darling Jean's time and although he probably wasn't nearly as awful as we thought, and she certainly seemed to like him, our Spanish sojourn wasn't the same that summer. Linda and I both married shortly afterwards and although in our letters we always promised to pay Aunt Jean a visit sometime soon, the years rolled by and the letters became just Christmas cards with increasingly brief notes enclosed. She only returned to England twice more, to attend the funerals of her parents, and although she invited us to visit we never got round to it, being tied up with our kids, jobs and suchlike.

Then the Ogre finally died in October of 2016 at the ripe old age of eighty-seven. Aunt Jean wrote to us after the funeral and Linda and I promised to visit her the following Easter. When I phoned to tell her we'd booked the tickets – plane not coach – she was delighted, but she died of a heart attack in March at the age of seventy-nine. A Dutch friend who will soon be introduced found her, made the necessary calls, and Aunt Jean's lawyers took over proceedings, including the funeral, which took place quickly, as per her instructions. It was one of the lawyers who phoned on that fateful evening, after which I rushed out to the garage to tell Paul to cut short his indoor cycling session and hear the sad but advantageous tidings. He stopped his infernal whirring for long enough to hear me out, before insisting on completing his hour of self-inflicted torture. At fifty-nine he still pounded the pedals along his beloved Staffordshire lanes, unless it was dark or raining, when he pounded them on his contraption in the garage, anxious to stay fit enough to keep up with his younger clubmates, mostly young whippersnappers in their forties and fifties.

After his shower we settled down to discuss the possible consequences of the lawyer's revelation.

"There's not much point talking about it till you've spoken to Linda," he said, looking rosy and relaxed. "She might be miffed about not getting the house. Why do you think your aunt left it to you anyway?"

"Oh, I think I was always her favourite and I wrote to her a bit more than Linda." I frowned. "But I suppose it's up to the two of us what we do with our, er... inheritance."

"Call her."

"I will, but first of all, how do you feel about having a house in Spain?"

"That's like asking me how I feel about having a... a carbon road bike."

I groaned. He always had cycling on the brain after he'd been cycling, even in the garage. "Please explain."

He rubbed his hands together. "Well, you know how I hate the new-fangled things and how I always preferred steel frames, until I discovered titanium."

"I recall your expensive discovery of titanium bikes, yes, but what's that got to do with Spain?"

He rubbed his nose, the only fleshy thing on his body, or upper body. "Spain's just not a place I'm interested in. I know a lot of folk like it, and good for them, but I've no desire to own a house there." He pointed at the phone. "See if Linda wants it and you keep the cash. Then we can have lots of nice holidays wherever we want."

Our summer holidays were the only time that Paul kissed his bikes goodbye and we'd travelled to some lovely places over the years, but never to Spain, as he thought it a somewhat crass destination. At the time he had a well-paid position in an engineering company and I was due to retire from my English teaching job at the local secondary school that summer.

I gazed at him sternly. "I've said it before and I'll say it again, you have snobbish misconceptions about Spain. You'd love it where Aunt Jean lives… lived. It's nothing like the coast and the roads must be wonderful for cycling. They were ever so quiet when we used to go."

He shook his glistening head. "Yes, and they were quiet here in the 1970s too. No, when you go you'll find that it's all changed now, for the worse. It'll have been built up and invaded by foreigners, all tearing around in their big cars."

I pictured the sleepy village basking in the summer sun. "I can't see it somehow. It's quite a way from the coast, you know."

"How far?"

"Oh, at least twenty miles, I'd say, and on the other side of the mountains. The roads are really winding too. When we went down to the beach at a place called Villajoyosa it took ages in her little car."

He sighed and smiled patiently. "Well, we've both seen programmes about how the sunseekers get everywhere these days. I bet your aunt's village has been ruined by them now."

"Well, we'll see in a couple of weeks, won't we?"

"Yes, you will."

"You could come, you know, given the, er… new circumstances."

"No, we've a lot of work on at the moment and it's better that the two of you go alone anyway. Take some photos and we'll talk about it when you come back. You'd better call Linda."

"Yes."

"I'll make a pot of tea."

Linda took my momentous news quite calmly, as the lawyer had called her too.

"Oh, right, he didn't say he was going to."

She chuckled. "He seems like a discreet man. Speaks good English too."

"Yes. It's sad about Aunt Jean, isn't it?"

"Yes, and just when we were finally going to see her. I feel guilty now."

"Me too." I paused respectfully. "So, what do you think about this will business?"

She sighed. "Well, I suppose we'll have to look into that on our trip instead of seeing her. There'll be a lot of things to sort out."

"Yes, he told me that too." I sipped my tea and glanced over at Paul. His expression was serene and attentive. I made an executive decision. "Look, Linda, I know the will says what it says about the house and things, but I think we should go there with open minds and decide what to do once we've seen what's what," I said, having always been a straight talker where financial matters are concerned.

She chuckled. "And how open is your mind about it?"

"Er, wide open. Look, Paul's not especially interested in having a house in Spain and it doesn't seem fair that she's left it to me anyway."

Linda giggled, her being one of those eternally cheerful people. "Ah, yes, well, but she might have millions in the bank, so the will might suit me just fine."

"I doubt it. She said years ago that the Ogre would be leaving his land to his son."

"I'm joking, Sue."

"What does Bill say about this?" I asked, referring to her not overly energetic husband who had recently retired from the bank where he'd worked for decades. In many ways Bill is the antithesis of Paul, being overweight and disdainful of physical exercise, but he is something of an amateur intellectual, a claim my husband cannot make, unless you count knowing every Tour de France winner since the race began and many other fascinating cycling facts.

"Bill made the right noises, then said he'd be done shortly. I'm still waiting for him to emerge from his study."

"Will he want a house in Spain?"

Linda shrugged. (Yes, we were on the phone, but we know each other remarkably well.) "Who knows? As long as he's got his books and computer he doesn't really mind where he is."

"Paul doesn't want to come with us at Easter to see our new acquisition."

"I don't think Bill will either. I don't mind. It's our business anyway."

"Yes, and Linda, as far as I'm concerned we can share and share alike."

She chuckled. "I've got you worried about the millions she might have, haven't I?"

"Oh, well..."

"I'm joking, silly. Let's just go and see what we think when we get there."

"Yes, we might just feel like selling up and clearing out."

"Hmm, we might, but it used to be lovely there, didn't it?"

"Yes, until the Ogre spoilt our fun. Paul says it'll be ruined now anyway."

"What does that cycling maniac know?"

I gazed at him. "Yes, what does that cycling maniac know?" I stuck out my tongue. "Speak soon then."

"Yes, bye, Sue."

I sipped my tea.

Paul smiled wryly. "So, you've already given away half of your aunt's house."

"What else could I do? Maybe Aunt Jean made her will that way to keep things simple."

"Yes, you should just sell up and split the proceeds." A gust of wind drove the incessant rain onto the French windows. "You can't beat England anyway."

I grinned fiendishly, for me. "We'll see about that."

"Yes, I've a feeling we will."

# 2

Rather than trying to weave a lot of mundane stuff skilfully into the story, I think I'll just get it over with now. In 2017 I was fifty-eight, fairly slim, of average height, with long greying hair and brown eyes. Paul was and still is five-eleven, too thin but very fit, with short, receding grey hair and blue eyes. Linda was sixty, a bit chubbier than me, but otherwise very similar. Bill was sixty-five, shortish, quite stout, with unruly grey wavy hair and sharp brown eyes. Physically only one aspect of one of us has changed since then, but I'll save that for later.

Paul and I have two children. Adam was then thirty-four and working for a big marketing company in London. He and his wife Emily live near Luton with their two small children, a boy and a girl. Our daughter Emma was thirty and recently separated from a long-term boyfriend. She was working for the Youth Hostel Association as a roving interim manager and troubleshooter, so we never quite knew where she was from one month to the next. Linda and Bill's son Luke was thirty-three and just as hard to pin down as our Emma, as was his current occupation, because since leaving university with a poor degree he'd worked as a builder's labourer, waiter, canal operative, council dustman, other miscellaneous things and, on and off during all this time, a language tutor, as he'd studied French and Spanish during his four dissipated years in Aberystwyth.

That then was the family panorama when Linda and I drove to the village from Alicante Airport in a stylish but chronically underpowered Fiat 500 on Wednesday 12th April 2017.

"The hills haven't changed at all," I said as I steered the car round the umpteenth bend since leaving the coastal road behind.

"No, they must have escaped any bad forest fires around here. The road's wider though."

"And smoother, and a bit busier, but not much. I think Paul was wrong about everything having changed for the worse," I said, although if we'd chosen another road past Guadalest I'd have seen that the scruffy village by an emerald green reservoir – just ten years old at the time – had been transformed into a tacky tourist destination overrun by cars, coaches and trippers. Fortunately we missed that blot on the sierra, while Sella, the only village we passed on the interminable climb, didn't seem much changed, as I pointed out to Linda.

"Hmm, I think it's a bit whiter and tidier now and there are about ten times more cars around, but it still looks much the same from what I can see of it."

"I hope our village hasn't changed much either."

She chuckled. "Our village?"

"Well it might become our village, in a manner of speaking. Uh-oh, looks like the weather's closing in."

The largely sunny sky had clouded over since we'd left the coast and when we drove into the mist the mountains suddenly seemed very forbidding.

"Aunt Jean said it sometimes snowed up here in winter," Linda said.

I flicked on the lights and wipers and slowed to a crawl. "Yes, it was nearly always hot and sunny when we came."

"She said it was quite hard to make a living around here. That's why a lot of the young people were leaving back then."

"Right. Er, why do you mention that now?"

She chuckled. "I don't know really. Maybe because it looks so grim. This was a holiday playground for us, but it must be different if you live here all the time."

As I began to negotiate the hairpin bends down the other side, a people carrier with German plates approached and passed. "He should put his lights on," I said, but a moment later I saw why he hadn't got around to it, as we suddenly pierced through the low cloud and began to discern the inland valley through the pine trees. As I drove on down, grateful for the power steering that I'm sure Aunt Jean's Dyane didn't have, we caught tantalising glimpses of several small villages before Aunt Jean's was suddenly there before us in all its rustic glory.

"I think it's a tiny bit bigger now," said Linda.

"And neater."

"And there are more cars, but it's not so different really."

"No, I'm glad," I said, looking forward to calling Paul and telling him how wrong he'd been. "I'll park and we'll ask someone where the hotel is."

"Er, do you remember any Spanish?"

I chuckled. "We never did know much." I parked alongside a scruffy little park and we climbed out. "The three of us always seemed to make our own fun."

She smiled. "I've been swotting up a bit."

"Me too, but you ask someone."

"Why me?"

"You're my big sister. You're responsible for me."

She asked a pleasant middle-aged lady who explained with words and gestures where the hotel was, so we grabbed our bags and found the modest place on a familiar street. The sombre young man there addressed us in English and showed us to a twin room with a good view of nearby woods and the mountains to the west.

"So you stay for three nights, yes?"

"Er, yes, but we might want to stay for longer," I said, finding that I didn't wish to broach the subject of Aunt Jean with a stranger.

He smiled. "No problem. Quiet now after the Easter." He stood scratching his head for a moment. "Er, can I inform Anke that you come?"

"Who is Anke?"

"Anke is friend of gin," I understood him to say.

"So am I," said Linda with a titter.

This perplexed him. "You too *friend* of Gin?"

"Gin, vodka, rum. Anything except whisky."

He shook his head. "No, I not mean gin, I mean Gin, your, er... family."

"Ah, you mean our Aunt Jean?" I said.

He smiled weakly. "Yes, the old lady, now dead. You are family, yes?"

"We're her nieces," Linda said.

He nodded uncomprehendingly.

I smiled. "She was our aunt, er... tante, er..."

"Tía!" Linda cried, making us both jump. "Aunt Jeeeen es... oh, what the hell's the word for our... tía."

He sighed. "OK, she aunt, so you her nices."

"Nieces," I corrected, ever the teacher.

"Nieces. And if you men?"

"We're not men," Linda snapped. "Do we look like men?"

"No, no..."

"Nephew is the word for niece if you are a man," I clarified.

Linda was now leafing through her tiny dictionary. "Er... sobrino. Right, nosotros estamos sobrinos de Jean."

He smiled. "Vosotras *sois* sobrin*as* de Gin."

Linda's brow creased. "OK, now, nosotras *sois* sobrin*as* de Jean."

He shook his close-cropped head. "No, you say, nosostras *somos* sobrinas de Gin."

She frowned. "That's not what you said."

He shrugged and eyed the doorway.

"We need to study the verbs, Linda."

She snorted, then tittered, as she rarely stayed annoyed for long.

I turned to our host. "So, who is… oh, I've forgotten the name now."

He smiled. "Anke. Anke is friend of your Aunt Gin."

"Ah, do you mean the Dutch lady?"

He frowned. "No, she not Deutsche, she from Holland."

"No, no, Dutch means..." Linda began, until I nipped the back of her arm. "Ow!"

"Sorry, no more linguistic gymnastics for now." I turned to the poor young man. "Yes, Anke from Holland. We would like to see her, please."

He looked relieved. "I call her now." He left.

We unpacked our small travel bags and lay down on our beds, lamenting the lack of a kettle.

"Perhaps this Anke lady will explain why we weren't told about the funeral in time," Linda murmured.

"All will be revealed, no doubt."

I was just nodding off to the sound of my sister's light snoring when the bedside phone rang.

"Yes?"

"Anke here," the man said. "She to come up?"

"No, we to come down, in five minutes."

"OK."

Anke proved to be a deeply tanned, short-haired, fit-looking lady in her sixties. Like most Dutch folk she spoke excellent English and, it transpired, pretty good Spanish too. After shaking our hands and sombrely expressing her sorrow for our loss, she whisked us off to a nearby bar. It was about seven o'clock by this time and although it was still light, it was far too chilly to sit at the single table outside.

"This place has changed a lot," said Linda when the young waitress had brought our coffees.

"It was very scruffy forty years ago," I said.

"It was quite scruffy seven years ago when Rik and I came here, but they have reformed it since then."

It turned out that Anke was from Rotterdam and lived in the village while her husband Rik tried in the vain to bring his career as a roving dredger to a close.

"His work in Dubai was to be his last project, but his boss begged him to go to Zanzibar to supervise a job, then another one came up in Qatar, and so it goes on, for the last two years. He comes home, then goes again for weeks at a time." She shrugged. "The money is useful, I suppose, but enough is enough."

"Is that why you're so tanned, Anke, after living in places like that?" Linda asked.

"Yes, before I worshipped the sun, but now only a little." She rubbed her rather wrinkled cheeks, then smiled. "So will you come to live here now?"

"Who knows?" said Linda brightly.

I cleared my throat. "Now we just want to take care of all the legal things. The lawyer seemed very efficient."

Anke frowned. "Yes, very. I saw your aunt a lot after her husband died. I live on the same street and we had often chatted, but it was only after he died that I began to visit her. She was quite fit for her age and the heart attack was unexpected. I arrived one day for tea as usual and found her in her chair, already quite cold. I called the ambulance and then found her papers in her desk drawer, where she'd told me they were. I called the lawyer and they told me they were the, er... albaceas, how do you say? The people in charge of the... testimony."

"The executors of the will," I said.

"Yes, sorry, I don't know words like that in English. So, a young man came quite soon and told me that the funeral would take place within two days, as is the law, unless there is a need to, er... embalsamar."

"Embalm?" I said, sitting in stiff imitation of an embalmed body.

"Yes, and as the doctor saw no reason for an autopsy, that is what happened."

"The lawyer told us she was cremated in Alcoy," said Linda.

"That's right. Me and three more ladies went to the little ceremony there, and then she was cremated."

"Only four people?" Linda said.

"Where are the ashes?" I asked simultaneously.

She smiled. "The lawyers have the ashes, I think." She sighed. "I had a key to her door – just in case, she told me – but the lawyer took it away after allowing me to empty the fridge and clean up in the kitchen."

"Thank you, Anke. We're seeing him tomorrow, or one of them," I said, pleased that Aunt Jean had given them clear instructions. They'd charge us the earth, no doubt, but had she not appointed them executors it might have been a very complicated business and we'd probably have been ripped off somewhere along the line anyway, I thought at the time. Holding on to her ashes seemed like going beyond the call of duty and their thoroughness clearly annoyed Anke, but she was merely a friend after all.

"Only four people at the funeral?" Linda repeated.

"Well, five if you include the lawyer, who came near the end. Your aunt was a quiet person in her later years, spending her days looking after her husband, who was ill for a long time. After he died she saw few people except me and the ladies in the bakery and the grocery shop. They came to the crematorium with me in my car."

"What was her husband like?" Linda asked.

"Old Juan?" She sighed. "A nice man, I think, but never outside much since me and Rik arrived. She told me they had been very happy and that she had no regrets."

Linda looked as guilty as I felt. We'd allowed our first, selfish impressions of the Ogre to colour our judgment and gone on to find more entertaining ways to spend our summers. In our defence I must say, as it isn't my intention to come across as a heartless so-and-so, that Aunt Jean was never especially persistent in her invitations, knowing, I think, that her husband didn't really want a couple of monolingual foreign women around for two or three weeks. Her invitations to her brother, our now deceased father, were even more lukewarm, so it has to be said that her splendid isolation was of her own choosing. We just settled for letters, as people often do, and the years rolled by.

Just then the chap from the hotel approached the doorway, but on seeing us I think he changed his mind and continued homeward or to the other bar. Anke ordered another coffee and Linda and I opted for red wine. We ended up eating a light dinner there and Anke shared a few of Aunt Jean's nostalgic stories with us. For many years she'd been a keen painter, often to be seen about the place with her easel and bright clothes, though she'd also driven into the hills to draw and paint. She'd sold quite a lot of pictures until about the turn of the century, after which she'd painted less and mainly for pleasure.

"You will see some of her paintings when you get the keys. Your aunt told me that Juan was a very traditional farmer, spending long days on his land, while she, his eccentric foreign wife, she said, did her own thing. I think she got on well with the local people, but never really fitted in. She didn't gossip much with the other ladies, so she was always an outsider, but I don't think she minded that."

"Did she speak good Spanish?" Linda asked.

"Oh, yes, very good, and even Valenciano, which the local people speak. She and I usually spoke in English, as she liked to speak it, not having many other opportunities."

Linda and I exchanged another guilty look.

Anke raised her coffee cup, so we clinked it with our glasses.

"To your aunt."

"To Aunt Jean," we said.

"But now you have the house, and I hope you will come to live here."

"I like it here," said Linda.

"It's too soon to say," I said. "My husband and I still work, you see."

"You finish in July," Linda said.

"Yes, but Paul doesn't."

"How old is he?" Anke asked.

"Nearly sixty."

She rubbed her hands together briskly, as if ridding them of dust. "Ha, enough work then, I think. Life is cheap here, the weather is good and the people pleasant. The north of Europe is so cold, expensive and busy."

"Yes, but Paul likes his job, as I think your husband likes his."

She frowned and growled comically. "Yes, but enough. Rik is a good photographer. Retire and take pictures, I say, but it's always one more job. His father was a dredger on the canals of Holland, you see, so it's in his blood. Does your husband have any hobbies at all?"

"One big hobby," I said. Paul hated me to refer to it as a mere hobby, although for the life of me I couldn't think of another word for it. "Cycling."

"Cycling? Oh, this is a cycling paradise, Sue! Kilometres and kilometres of quiet roads, up and down all the valleys in the sunshine all day long! Here he would be in heaven."

I made a mental note of this enthusiastic outburst for future reference.

"Does your husband have a hobby, Linda?"

She chuckled. "He has his studies, mostly history, but also other things. He just needs a desk, shelves and a power supply."

"Oh, well here he can study to his heart's contentment, Linda! The street is very quiet and the rooms at the back of the house even quieter. This place is *perfect* for studying, all day and all night if he desires."

Anke was clearly rather keen for us to move into our aunt's house, so I asked her if she had many friends here.

She pursed her rather thin lips. "Hmm, friends, well, I get on fine with the local people, and also most of the foreigners, but I suppose my two true friends are in Holland. They come to visit every year and I also visit them. Here I have a lot of acquaintances, shall we say? In some ways I'm like your aunt. I speak to the ladies here, but I don't become involved in their lives." She sighed. "What I want is for my Rik to be here all the time."

"Of course. Do you have any hobbies?" I asked, as it had irked me slightly that she'd only asked about our husbands' pastimes.

"Oh, I read and walk and I like cooking, the usual things. And you two?"

"The same," said Linda. "And a bit of gardening."

"Oh, the house has no garden, only a small patio."

"But I'm happy with a few pot plants," she said, not really being all that green-fingered.

I had to admit that I liked doing the usual things too, so maybe she was right in deducing that it was the men who'd be the hobbyists. Anke asked for the bill, but I insisted on paying, and we soon stepped out onto the deserted street.

Anke proffered her hand, but before I could grasp it she elected to slap her forehead instead. "Oh, but you haven't seen the house yet!"

"Has it changed?" Linda asked.

"I expect so. Come with me and I'll show you, from outside at least."

"OK"

I suppose Linda and I had put off viewing the house out of respect for Aunt Jean, as we'd preferred to hear Anke's tales about her rather than rushing off to see what she'd left us. It's at the end of a row of three-storey houses and is a little wider than the others. We saw that the previously off-white facade had been rendered and painted a tasteful peach colour, probably some time ago, but it looked quite presentable in the dim light of the street lamp. The wooden blind covering the entire doorway was a bit flaky, as were the ones behind the fine black metal bars on the two ground-floor windows.

"Is it very old inside?" Linda asked quietly.

"Quite old, yes, but always clean. Some foreigners would have the whole house renovated from bottom to top, but I don't think that is necessary. It would lose its charm, I think. Our house is similar inside, but a little smaller." She led us onto a narrow track to see the side of the house, which had one barred window on the ground floor and two unbarred ones on the other two. "It is very deep, you see, and bigger than it looks from the front. Here the rendering is a little cracked because it gets more sun."

We must have seemed a little melancholy, because Anke didn't pursue the subject of renovation, instead inviting us to her house for a drink.

"Can we come tomorrow, Anke, after we've seen the lawyer?" I said.

"We're a little tired now," said Linda, despite her snooze.

"Yes, good idea. I'll be in all afternoon."

We saw her to her house and she unlocked the stout door. "In the light of day you will see how you feel about your house."

"Yes, I think we will," I said.

We said goodnight and strolled down the silent street.

"Can you imagine living here?" I murmured.

"Hmm, I don't know. I can imagine spending time here though. What about you?"

"I don't know yet. I want to get all the tiresome stuff over with first."

"Yes, me too."

# 3

The tiresome stuff began at eleven o'clock the next morning, about an hour after the lawyer arrived. After handing us the plain copper urn and expressing his condolences, he whisked us off to the house, handed me a bunch of keys, and said he was going for a coffee.

"I think he's done this sort of thing before," said Linda as I unlocked the door.

"Yes, probably with other foreigners."

As the heavy door swung open the slightly musty air assailed our nostrils, so we lost no time in pulling up the blinds and opening the single-pane windows. Apart from a light layer of dust the place looked clean and we saw that it was simply furnished. Gone was the dark, heavy furniture that we'd known, replaced by lighter, tasteful items that had seen plenty of use. The floor tiles were large and of a reddish hue, and on going upstairs we saw that every inch of the floor was the same, including the stairs, except those tiles were smaller. Almost all of the walls were painted a very light shade of yellow and we agreed that Aunt Jean hadn't bothered her head too much about interior decoration.

"She had good taste, but she wasn't adventurous," I said.

"I guess she put her art into her art rather than the house," Linda said, and we then began to examine her paintings, of which there were one or two in each room, except the large ground-floor sitting room, where there were four. They were all landscapes and pictures of the village and other villages, done in oils and watercolours. They seemed very good to our untrained eyes. Her studio was on the top floor overlooking the mountains we'd driven through, now bathed in sunlight. An old easel was leaning against a wall and all her paints and brushes were stored neatly in drawers. There were half a dozen canvases leaning against another wall and not a spot of paint on the floor.

"I think she must have given it up some time ago," I said.

"Yes, there are a lot of stairs for an old lady, although she must have got up here to clean. How many bedrooms are there?"

On the top floor there were two large, almost empty bedrooms, plus the studio, while the second floor boasted a master bedroom, another with a double bed but no other furniture, a third smaller, empty one and a bathroom with a standard white suite, including a bidet. The ground floor housed a functional kitchen, furnished in the 1990s, we guessed, a small bathroom with a shower cubicle, a small parlour and the large sitting room.

"A man could just move in here," I said. "To the masculine eye there's nothing wrong with the place."

Linda chuckled. "*I* could just move in here. A lot of it's like a blank canvas, and the bits that are filled in aren't too bad."

"I expected it to be old and dark and full of stuff, the accumulations of a long life."

"I reckon Aunt Jean remained young at heart, and she never was all that bothered about stuff."

"She had plenty of books though." I pointed to the shelves in the sitting room, which on closer inspection contained lots of novels in English, some in Spanish, and a long row of expensive art books. In one corner of the room there was a two-foot high slightly phallic wooden sculpture, but very few other ornaments.

Linda, meanwhile, had found the back-door key and was exploring the rear patio, enclosed by high rendered walls.

"Look, Sue, the pot plants I mentioned are already here. It must've rained since she died, as they're not looking too bad. I'll water them later."

I scuffed the ground with a lightly shod foot. "Ha, the tiles are the same as inside. They must have bought a job lot."

"I wonder when the Ogre came to live here. She never said in her letters to me."

I perched on an old wicker chair. "When they got married, I suppose, about two years after our last visit. He doesn't seem to have made much of a mark on the place," I said, as I'd seen no typically male artefacts around the place. There was a single photograph of them in the sitting room, probably taken about twenty years ago among blossoming almond trees. They looked healthy and wore contented smiles. We agreed that he must have softened with age, as he'd been quite curt and sullen that summer when he'd appeared on the scene.

We'd just begun to nosey around in their bedroom when the lawyer called up the stairs.

"Coming!" I cried.

"His clothes seem to have gone, apart from this old jacket," Linda said from the wardrobe.

"Maybe she gave them away. We'll have to ask Anke." (She later told us that she'd taken them to a charity shop in Alcoy. Aunt Jean had sold their car after he died, her poor eyesight having put her off driving. This was also the reason she'd given up painting, Anke believed.)

"What do you think of the place?" I asked my sister.

"I love it. And you?"

"I like it. Oh, well, we'd better get started on all the tiresome stuff."

As the brisk young lawyer will play little part in this account I'll just summarise our business with him during the next few days. Aunt Jean had left the house and contents to me and about €28,000 in savings to Linda, although inheritance tax would have to be paid on the total estimated amount. Aunt Jean's will had been made in February, not long after we'd confirmed our Easter visit, but he was unable or unwilling to discuss any previous wills. The following morning a young lady in some way connected with the lawyers' office drove us to the police station to get the NIE numbers which every foreigner who owns or inherits property in Spain must have, before helping us to open bank accounts in Alcoy. Two days' later we visited the lawyers' office one last time and our man assured us that they would take care of everything and that the taxes would be calculated, the money requested, and the ownership of the house notarised.

"That's good," I said. I gazed around his plush office. "How much will all this cost?"

He looked puzzled. "The office furniture?"

Linda burst out laughing.

"No, your services."

He frowned thoughtfully. "It's hard to say exactly, but it will be very reasonable, I assure you. We value our foreign clients and for this reason provide auxiliary services to enable you to take possession of the house and money."

"Do you value us more than your Spanish clients?" my daft sister asked.

His lips twitched. "Exactly the same. We have an excellent reputation."

I cleared my throat. "Er, Linda and I want to be joint owners of the house and, er... the money. Can you help us with that too?"

"Yes, but one thing at a time. First the inheritance, then we can help you with further affairs if you wish. As for the money, that will be your business."

"Good, yes, thanks. Until, er... when then?"

"Are you in a hurry to take possession of the house?"

"Yes," said Linda.

"No," said I. "I mean, there's no mad rush."

"Mad rush?"

"There's no big hurry. Will it all be done by the summer?"

"Oh, certainly. Please email to tell me when you are coming and we will arrange an appointment with the notary then." He stood up and extended his hand.

"One more question," Linda said.

He withdrew his hand and sat down.

"Can we keep the keys until we go, two days from now?"

He frowned. "Hmm, that is a little unregular (sic)."

"We won't steal the house, we promise."

He smiled for the first time. "Americans have been known to take castles from Europe to their country, you know."

"Yes, but we've only got one cabin bag each."

They had a little chuckle, so I joined in. I think the chap was pretty humourless really, but Linda has a way of making people loosen up.

"All right then. Please leave the keys at the hotel. I will be over there again next week."

"Has another foreigner popped their clogs?" she said.

"Popped their what?"

"She means died," I said.

He assumed a poker face. "That is highly confidential." He smiled, sprang up, shook our hands and ushered us out.

"Can you never be serious, Linda?" I muttered on the stairs.

"What for? Life's too short to go around with long faces. Come on, let's have a drink in that nice square we saw."

Apart from the legal stuff we spent the week pottering around the house, village and surrounding area and we saw Anke several times. She insisted on looking after the six pot plants, so we carted them round to her patio, also taking a peek at her house, which was smarter than she'd suggested and expensively furnished. On our final evening we invited her to dinner at the bar – the other bar being rather scruffy and usually full of men – but we arranged to meet her at Aunt Jean's house first. When I ushered her in Linda was putting the finishing touches to our impromptu art exhibition in the sitting room.

"Anke," I announced a little nervously. "We'd like you to take two of these paintings. They're the ones that were upstairs in the studio. We thought you might like to have a landscape and also one of the village. Please take whichever you want."

A smiling Linda stood unnaturally erect with her arms folded, looking like a museum curator about to be consigned to the loony bin.

"Oh, that's so kind of you, Sue, Linda," she said with emotion. "I would very much like to have that one of the mountain in the mist, if that's all right."

"Of course, and choose one of the village too."

She smiled. "I already have one. It's in our bedroom, now framed. Your aunt gave it to me only a short time before she died. I will treasure them both."

She kissed us on both cheeks for the first time, before she and Linda carried out the large picture. I double locked the door and patted it. Aunt Jean's ashes would remain in her house until our return.

Later in the bar.

"So, have you decided how you will use the house?" Anke asked us after we'd polished off our tapas and a bottle of white wine.

"It depends partly on what our husbands say," I said.

She smiled. "Partly?"

"Yes, we've decided that we're definitely going to keep it."

"And come to stay in it," Linda added helpfully.

"But whether we'll just come for holidays or to… for longer does depend on them," I said, as although I'd waxed lyrical about the brilliant cycling roads when I'd called Paul, I'd refrained from speaking about when he might be riding on them.

"Yes, of course, if your husband will still be working. What about you, Linda?"

"I spoke to Bill. He wants to come in summer." She looked at me. "I think we'll all be coming in summer."

"Yes, we will," I said, as although Paul had been reading up on Norway and enthusing about the fjords, I was determined to veto that idea and insist on holidaying in our new house.

"There is plenty of room there for two couples," Anke said.

We agreed that there was.

"What about your children? Our son Marc comes every year with his wife and daughter. They love it here. The village pool is very good. It opens in June."

We'd already told her something about my Adrian and Emma and Linda's Luke. I guessed that Adrian would have other plans and that Emma would be busy putting ailing Youth Hostels to rights, but the footloose Luke was another matter.

"I doubt mine will be able to come this summer," I said.

"I never know what my son's going to do," said Linda.

"I think just the four of us should come first," I said, as although Luke is a charming young chap I feared that the prospect of a rent-free property might prove to be an opportunity he'd be unable to resist, given the chance.

Linda, who almost always knows what I'm thinking, agreed that the oldies would first take possession and stake claims to their living and sleeping space, before inviting the youngsters to avail themselves of the guest quarters. I suspected she'd say that, but still felt relieved. You'll see why in due course.

Anke ordered our coffees and liqueurs – Linda and I had said very little in Spanish all week – before asking us how long we planned to stay during our next visit.

"Two weeks, I suppose," I said. "Paul won't be able to get longer off work."

"No, but you could stay for more time, no?"

"Er, I hadn't really thought about that."

"I had," said Linda. "The three of us could stay for a month."

"What about your job?" I said, as she'd worked as a part-time bookkeeper at a small travel firm since leaving a larger company where she'd spent many years.

She made a dismissive gesture with her hand which she might have seen some Spaniards do, as it was new to me. "I think I'll kick that into touch soon."

"Really?"

"Yep." She laughed. "You don't think I'm going to go on working after you retire, do you?"

"I though you liked it. You said it was easy work and got you out of the house."

"Well now the house here will get me out of the house back home, won't it?" She sipped her apple liqueur and sighed. "I'd always expected to retire at sixty anyway, till the government decided to treat us like mere men."

While Linda and Anke discussed the merits of the non-working life – Anke had been a nurse in Holland until her husband's lucrative overseas work had ended her career many years ago – I sipped my almond liqueur and began to feel a bit jealous. Linda and Bill would be free to come and go while I'd remain by my husband's side until he finally decided to retire, as I thought it a bit selfish to spend much time in Spain without him. I thought about all the quiet, picturesque roads we'd seen during the last week and imagined him riding along them in the benign sunshine.

"...*so* lively in July and August," Anke was saying. "The other foreigners and some locals sometimes have guests and the hotel is usually full, so there's a good atmosphere. The summer pass for the swimming pool is cheap for residents. It's just as good as any hotel pool and there are rarely too many children. Yes, you will like it very much, I think."

I butted in. "Anke, do you think it'll be too hot for cycling in summer?"

"Hmm, well, at midday I think so, yes, but if he sets off early in the morning he can do a good ride before it gets too hot."

"Hmm, good."

"And then relax his tired legs in the pool. When we first came here we looked at expensive houses in the countryside with pools, but when we visited the municipal pool we saw there was no need to have our own, so we preferred to buy a house in the village, to be more sociable and make it easier to learn Spanish."

Anke clearly considered the local pool to be her trump card, as although she hadn't mentioned it much until then – it was looking a bit scruffy and desolate at the time – she was now playing it with a vengeance. Why, I wondered, was she so incredibly eager for us to come?

"What are the other foreigners like here?" I asked her.

She pursed her lips and thought for a while. "Well, you saw the French lady one day. She and her husband are very quiet and we don't see much of them. There is also a Belgian man who I think might have split up with his wife, as I haven't seen her for a while, then there is the English couple I think I mentioned."

"Yes, what are they like?" Linda asked.

"Oh, quite young, in their forties, I think. They have a chalet just outside the village, beyond the, er... residual waters place." She held her nose.

"The sewage works?" I said.

"Yes, the sewage works. Their house is maybe two hundred metres from there. Another liqueur?"

We nodded and she ordered three more tiny glasses.

"Yes, but what are they *like*, this English couple?" Linda insisted.

I sensed that Anke was trying not to pull a face. "Oh, you'll see. I think they are away right now, but they sometimes come here in the evenings."

"Do you not like them?" said the straight talker.

"Well, Linda, I don't like to say bad things about people. I'm not a gossip and everyone has a right to live their life as they wish."

"And how do they live their lives?" she said, now in full inquisitorial mode.

Anke sighed. "In my opinion, in an unconventional manner, but it is none of my business. When I see them I say hello and nothing more."

"What sort of unconventional manner, Anke?"

"Linda, please drop the subject," I said.

Anke looked around the now deserted bar. "Look, they come and go a lot. When they are here they often have visitors, also from England, I think, who come in expensive cars and talk loudly."

"Oh, so are they posh?" Linda asked.

"No they are not posh, not at all posh. They have tattoos and speak strange, ugly English. They are common people, I think, but seem to have a lot of money. On one trip they had a Ferrari, on the next a Range Rover. They go away for weeks, then come back with their cars and friends and have big parties."

"They do sound a bit... irregular," I said.

Linda's brown eyes opened wide. "They sound like *gangsters* to me." She laughed heartily, but I failed to see the funny side.

"Do you think they're dangerous, Anke?"

She ran her tongue around her well-preserved white teeth and nodded slowly. "I sense that danger is part of their lives, but in the village they behave all right and don't bother anyone, apart from sometimes we hear their music if the wind is blowing this way. We don't worry about them, but we don't wish to know them. Rik thinks that one day there will be a police raid and we'll see no more of them. I ho... fear he might be right."

"They sound intriguing," said Linda.

Anke shrugged. "For me they are just a... a spot on the landscape here."

"A blot on the landscape," I corrected. "Oh, well, as long as they don't bother people I suppose it doesn't matter."

"Live and let live," said Linda.

Anke smiled and rubbed her hands together. "Those people are nothing to us. The village is wonderful, especially in summer. If Rik is here, which I think he will be, we will have a marvellous time."

Linda paid up and after stepping outside we agreed to keep in touch. We kissed and then waved when she was about to turn the corner.

"A nice lady," said Linda as we strolled back to the hotel.

"Maybe a bit lonely."

"She misses her Rik."

"Perhaps he really will retire soon."

"Perhaps Paul will retire soon."

I sighed. "Perhaps."

"I mean, it's not as if you need the money. You've got better pensions than us and this house is a real windfall. Anke thinks it's worth at least a hundred thousand, even now when prices are low, and there's the money Aunt Jean left us too. You ought to tell Paul that he can retire because the money he might have earned... well, he's been sort of gifted it."

"Are you a bit tipsy, Linda?"

She looked flushed under the hotel lights, but we had been sitting around in the sun quite a lot.

"No, just happy about all this. It's a great stroke of luck. Good old Aunt Jean."

I thought about the date of her will. "Yes, good old Aunt Jean."

"You know, when we get back I'm going to have a chinwag with Paul and make him see sense."

"You'll do no such thing."

"I'll be subtle."

"You'll be silent on the subject."

"But I don't want me and Bill to be out here if you can't come. It wouldn't be right, especially as she left the house to you."

"That's irrelevant. We agreed to share and share alike."

"That's true, and I appreciate it."

"Anyway, you leave Paul to me. I've already had a good idea."

"What?"

"You'll see. Come on, let's get to bed. We've an early start tomorrow."

# 4

The following Saturday evening we celebrated Paul's sixtieth birthday at home, just the four of us. After a pleasant meal which included my first attempts at making cod croquettes, fried goat's cheese and *patatas bravas*, Bill and Linda nipped out to their car to fetch the rather bulky present I'd bought Paul. Linda and I had driven to Stoke to get it and it would be the culmination of several days spent subtly praising the roads, landscape and climate of inland Alicante.

"Oh, what's that great big thing?" Paul said as they deposited the oblong object on the parquet floor.

"Unwrap it and see," I said.

He began to tear off the paper and his face almost fell. "Oh, is it some kind of suitcase?"

"You'll see."

"It's just what you need," said Linda.

"Every… man should have one," said Bill.

Paul gazed at the large round shapes on one side and smiled. "Oh, it's a bike box."

"It's a state of the art, hard-shell bike case, guaranteed to transport even the most expensive carbon or titanium bikes in safety," I said, replicating the shop owner's spiel. I almost added that it had cost me over three hundred pounds, but no doubt he'd find that out soon enough.

"Thanks a lot, love." He gave me a quick hug and kiss. "I planned to stick one of my old bikes in a box for our trip, but this is much better," he said, as the summer holiday was already a done deal.

"Just think, your first holiday for ages with your bike," Bill said, doubtless recalling the time we went to Italy and he hired one – just to go for a spin now and then, he'd said – and effectively turned me into a cycling widow for a fortnight.

"Yes, it'll be good to take a decent bike."

Linda sipped her cava and smiled. "And do you know what the chap in the shop said? He said that the folk who're always hopping off on cycling trips just fill the rest of the box with their clothes and only have to pay for one case. Isn't that clever?"

I gave her a warning look.

Paul gave her a serene look. "Linda, I've happily agreed to come to Spain in summer."

She clamped her lips shut and nodded.

"I must say this box makes me happier about taking my bike though. I'm looking forward to exploring the roads you've told me *so* much about, but what the future holds I can't say just yet. As you know, I've got a lot of responsibility at the firm and I've been thinking about sort of winding down over the next couple of years until someone else can fill my post, so I'd like to take things one step at a time."

(I ought to point out that he owned 12.5% of the company and had no plans to relinquish his share.)

"Quite right, Paul," said Bill, looking flushed after eating and drinking his fill, as always. "Don't let these infernal women nag you into doing anything you don't want to do."

Paul smiled. "No, Bill, I won't."

"As for me, well, I mean to enjoy the holiday and take a break from my studies."

"Are you still on the East India Company?" Paul asked.

He prodded his glasses. "I'm still on the *Dutch* East India Company, Paul. The British East India Company hasn't even been formed yet – in my studies, I mean – but I'm discovering some very interesting things that these so-called professional scholars appear to have overlooked."

"Anke and her husband might be interested in that," said Linda. "They're Dutch."

"Yes, I look forward to telling them about their history."

"Swot up on Dutch canals. I bet Rik will be interested in that," I said.

"Yes, I will. Hmm, yes, I suppose I'll take that old netbook of mine, in case I feel like doing a bit over there."

"There's no internet," I said.

He grinned. "I'll take a dongle, dear."

"I bet the first thing he'll do will be to find the best room for a study," said Linda.

Bill tutted. "No, a quiet corner will suffice." He glanced at Paul. "We might not like it as much as you two assume we will, you know. One mustn't look a gift horse in the mouth, of course, but there's no guarantee that this horse is the right, er… mount for us, if you see what I mean."

"Yes, Bill," I said.

"Like Paul, I mean to go with an open mind and weigh up the pros and cons of future, er… potentially longer sojourns on the Iberian Peninsula."

"Yes, Bill," Linda said.

He raised a chunky forefinger imperiously. "*But*, I do know that the Moors had a great impact on that area, long after the Christians kicked them out." He beamed at us. "Did you know that the irrigation systems still in use might well be the very same ones that they installed up to a thousand years ago?"

"Really?" I said.

"They must be a bit worn out then," said Linda.

Bill sighed. "They'll have received periodic maintenance, no doubt. Yes, I mean to get out and explore and take photos. I have a pal on a history forum who's very well up on that sort of thing, so I'd like to send him some shots to see what he makes of them."

"Er, Bill, I think you'll have to walk to see things like that," I said.

He chuckled and patted his considerable paunch. "I know, and I know you know that I'm not overly fond of stretching my legs, except in bed, but I think the time has come to reduce this belly of mine. Yes, I mean to start walking a lot more this summer."

"Why not start now?" Linda asked.

He puffed out his cheeks, then exhaled slowly. "Yes… yes, I might. Who wants a drop more cava?"

Over coffee we broached the subject of the Spanish language.

"…a Latin language, of course, like the others of Southern Europe, except Basque," Bill was saying. "Now, Basque is a fascina… ouch."

Linda had grasped his thigh. "Yes, dear, but we're not talking about that just now."

"I think the problem is that whoever speaks best tends to do all the talking," I said. "On our trip that was usually Anke, so we didn't practise much at all. I'll study a bit every day and in summer I'm going to try to speak to the locals."

"Me too," said Linda.

"I shall also set aside a little time for Spanish," said Bill.

"Hola, adios, gracias," said Paul.

"Very good, love, but there's a bit more to it than that."

"Not for me, not yet anyway. Oh, I'll learn a few more words, but I'll leave the talking to you."

I smiled. "You might meet some local cyclists and want to chat to them."

"Oh, no doubt they'll speak a bit of English."

I thought about the man at the hotel, the lawyer and his colleagues, and the people we'd dealt with in the bars and shops. "Hmm, you might be right, but that's no excuse. Anke speaks fairly well, I think, and if we end up spending more time there we'll want to communicate with the locals, won't we? A lot of them are quite old and I'm sure they don't speak English."

Paul yawned. "All in good time, love." He gazed fondly at his present. "Yes, I like the case. I'll put a bike in it tomorrow to see how well it fits."

"You do that, Paul," said Linda, before winking at me.

My last term of teaching passed fairly quickly and on the whole I was happy to retire. I felt satisfied with my long career and hadn't really suffered from the stress which seems to be endemic in the profession nowadays. I must say that the excessive paperwork and exams had become irksome, as had the unhealthy obsession with Ofsted reports, but I now look back on my years in the classroom with a certain pride. Linda resigned from her bookkeeping job at the end of June and immediately put her logistical skills into practice by listing the furniture and other bits and pieces we'd need to buy as soon as we arrived.

"I think we ought to buy two new mattresses and we'll need furniture for that second bedroom," she said one day in early July. "And two new easy chairs for the sitting room."

"I think we ought to wait till we get there, Linda."

"What, and spend the whole holiday roughing it and doing errands?"

"Hmm."

"When do you finish?"

"On the 21st of July."

"And Paul finishes on the 28th, doesn't he?"

"Yes." He had managed to get two and a half weeks holiday in the end and we had booked our flights accordingly.

"Look, why don't me and you go out a few days earlier and get the place shipshape, or shipshape-ish?"

"We could, but shouldn't they share the load?"

"There won't be any loads to speak of, as the delivery men will put things where we want them."

"I was speaking metaphorically, partly."

"Hmm, normally I'd agree with you, but we're the keenest about the house because we've been there. It's in our interests to make things go smoothly so they'll have a good time, especially Paul."

"Hmm."

"Unless Paul enjoys traipsing round furniture shops and other shops. Oh, and there's the notary appointment and other lawyer stuff too."

I pictured Paul assembling his bike, itching to hit the road. "All right, we'll see if we can change our flights and go a few days earlier."

"Bill might want to come then too."

"No," I said, more firmly than I'd intended. "No, it's not fair on Paul to have to travel alone."

She grinned. "Yes, you're right. Bill would only get under our feet anyway."

So it was that after liaising with the lawyer we flew to Spain on the Monday and drove our hire car straight to Alcoy, where he accompanied us to the notary's office and I took possession of my aunt's house. Back in his office the lawyer informed us that we'd have to pay a little under twelve thousand in inheritance task.

"That's a bit steep, Eduardo," said Linda.

"Steep?"

"Dear."

"You mean a lot?"

"Yes, mucho."

He smiled shrewdly. "It would have been more, but I managed to have the house valued at only sixty thousand. I have saved you at least three thousand."

"Gracias," Linda said.

"De nada, Linda."

"Cuánto, er… do we owe you?"

"The bill will be made and posted to you."

She narrowed her eyes. "Yes, but cuánto es, Eduardo, more or less?"

"Oh, a little over a thousand altogether, I think."

"That's fine," I said, as I'd expected it to be more. "We'll contact you about putting the house in both our names soon."

He smiled. "I am at your disposal, Sue. Please tell other foreigners about our services. Not all lawyers and assessors are as transparent as us."

"Will we get a discount if we do?" Linda asked.

He chuckled. "Yes, you might." He stood up. "It has been a pleasure to do business with you, ladies."

We shook hands and made for the door, but Linda wasn't done.

"Oh, Eduardo, hoy es soleado y hace calor," she said, meaning that it was sunny and hot today.

He grinned. "Es verdad. Hoy hace mucho calor. Adiós y buena suerte."

"Verdad means true and buena suerte means good luck," Linda said on the stairs.

"I know."

"You see, Sue, if you say something in Spanish they have to answer back in Spanish, even him."

"Yes, but I'm sure he knew it was hot and sunny without you telling him."

"No importa. It doesn't matter. Just say the first thing that comes into your head. Come on, let's get cracking. We've a lot to do."

The village looked splendid under the burning sun and the pine woods contrasted with the dry fields of mostly almond and olive trees. We were glad of the air conditioning in the car – an estate this time, to accommodate the bike case and anything bulky we bought – and were pleasantly surprised by the coolness of the house, although we soon found that the temperature rose gradually as we climbed the stairs to check that nothing had changed.

Back in the sitting room I suggested a bite to eat in the bar. By way of reply Linda brandished a dangling tape measure.

I groaned.

"There's no time to lose, Sue. We must order the furniture we need asap to make sure it arrives in time."

I snatched the tape measure, wound it in, and left it on the dusty windowsill. "Food and drink first, then a siesta. We've got all week."

I won't bore you with the details of the four tiresome and tiring days that followed. We cleaned the place from top to bottom, ordered some furniture online – using my tablet on the bar's Wi-Fi – and some from one of the many furniture shops in Alcoy. Linda preferred a large bedroom on the top floor, so we furnished that in pine, while I retained most of Aunt Jean's darker furniture in her room, though we bought a new mattress for the king-sized bed. We chose another upstairs bedroom for the only guest room and furnished that in pine too, storing the two spare mattresses for emergencies. We decided to leave Aunt Jean's studio as it was for the time being. On Saturday we did a big shop in a supermarket in Cocentaina, a smaller town slightly easier to reach than Alcoy, and that evening Anke and Rik returned from Holland. She'd gone to see their son and welcome her husband back from Bahrain, where he'd gone after Qatar, though he'd come back to Spain for a while between the two jobs.

As we both felt like a rest from the house that had kept us so busy, I called her and we met for dinner in the bar.

Rik proved to be a huge, bronzed man with muscly arms and receding silvery hair. He was friendly but didn't say much when we were updating Anke about house matters. Only when we asked him about his work did he open up and become quite talkative, so much so that Linda later said he was 'a bit of a barge bore', as he had gone into unnecessary detail about the dredging barges which he piloted. Over coffee Anke subtly steered the conversation onto the subject of our husbands' arrival.

"We've done all the hard work," said Linda. "There are some little DIY jobs for them to do, but other than that they can do as they please."

Anke mentioned the swimming pool and I told her that when we'd signed on the electoral roll at the village hall we'd bought four monthly passes for the pool.

"Ah, good, in summer the pool is an important part of our daily routine, although on Monday we're driving up to the north for a few days."

"Yes, you said you might," I said, quite pleased about having to fend for ourselves for a while. Anke had been ever so helpful on our first visit and we both enjoyed spending time with her, but I felt that it was preferable for us to find our feet alone rather than having someone 'in the know' around much of the time.

"I live in heat," said Rik, almost causing Linda to laugh. "When I come home I want to get out of it for a while. In Qatar the temperature reached fifty degrees some days. It was hard on the barge, I can tell you."

"Well it's been lovely to see you," said Linda, pushing away her cup and saucer. "When you get back you must tell us all about the north."

She called the waiter, but Rik insisted on paying, so we thanked them and agreed to meet up when they got back.

"That was nice, but I didn't get to say a word of Spanish," Linda grumbled as we made our way to the little park to enjoy the cooling breeze.

"Don't worry, you'll be the number one Spanish speaker from now on."

We sat on a bench among the trees and breathed in the fragrant air. We were alone and Linda was silent for once, so I mused on the events that had led up to our being there. Aunt Jean's ashes took pride of place on the mantelpiece above the wood-burning stove in the sitting room, although Linda was determined to find people who had known her and ask them where they thought she'd have liked them to be scattered. I'm what you might call a spiritual but not religious person and as I gazed at the starry sky I wondered if Aunt Jean might be up there looking down, pleased that her undeserving nieces had kept her house and meant to… what? Live there? Personally I already liked the idea and I knew that my sister felt the same, but it would all depend on what our other halves made of the house, village and country in which we had inadvertently found ourselves. Almost all expats think long and hard about where they choose to emigrate and many have to live with the consequences of their decision, having sold up back home, but we were in the privileged position of having been gifted a house and having no obligation to live in it. At that moment it felt like a peculiar state of affairs, but by the end of the holiday I believed we'd have a much clearer idea of what the future might hold.

"A penny for your thoughts," Linda eventually said.

"You always know what I'm thinking."

"It's fate, us being here."

"I'm not sure I believe in fate, Linda."

"What else can it be? I already feel at home here."

"Yes, well, I feel at home out here on this wonderfully starry night, but it won't always be like this."

She sighed. "Ah, qué será será, Sue. Tomorrow we pick up the boys and our new life will begin."

I decided to broach a subject that had been niggling me somewhat. "Yes, but although we see a lot of each other, we've never shared a house before. I mean, do you think that would be, er... practical, in the longer term?"

"Don't overthink things, Sue."

"No."

"Go with the flow."

"Yes."

"Because the fact is that both of us are facing a double-edged challenge."

"Are we?"

"Yes."

"What is it, or are they?"

"Can't you guess... Miss?"

"Oh, I see. You mean retiring *and* being here."

"Yes." She raised her hands and twisted them in a flamenco-style way. "That's why it's fate. Just when we were about to retire, this happened."

"Hmm, let's hope the boys feel the same."

"They will, you'll see."

I tapped the bench four times.

# 5

As I drove up from the coast towards Sella I could see Paul's eyes in the mirror, avidly viewing the sinuous, almost deserted road, before glancing around at his bike case in the back, then once more at the road. I left him to his reverie and asked Bill what he thought of it so far.

"Well, Sue, after the inevitable bustle of the airport and the busy motorway through decidedly arid countryside, I confess to having suspected that the old rose-tinted specs may have come into play when you and Linda described the delights that awaited us. Now that we're climbing away from the built-up coast and into these lovely green hills, however, I'm gradually becoming attuned to the tranquillity that you led me to expect," he said, never being one to use five words where fifty would do.

"I'm glad you like it."

"What do you think of it, Paul?" Linda asked over her shoulder.

"Twenty-one or maybe twenty-four," he mumbled.

"What?"

"Oh, sorry, I was just thinking about which sprocket I'd be using now. I love hills like this one. They're not too steep and you can get into a good rhythm. There's nothing like this in Staffordshire."

"Most of them are like this here," I said proudly, as if I'd made them. "And almost all of them are this quiet."

Unlike our first trip over the mountains at Easter, the sun was shining and when the cluster of villages came into view Bill began to shuffle around, taking it all in.

"All those places were Moorish settlements, I bet, or so the place names indicate. They had a fine civilisation here in Spain, with a lot of culture and tolerance. Then the Christians waded in and chucked them out unless they converted, which I suppose they pretended to do, but–"

"Did you bring a dongle?" I asked quickly.

"Oh, yes, I'm dongled up all right. I hope it works."

"Look, that's our village there with the woods behind it," said Linda.

"Very nice," said Paul, his eyes looking a bit glazed.

"Very compact," said Bill. "That's how the Moors preferred to build them."

Linda lowered her window and put out her hand. "Ooh, it's still hot and it's six o'clock. You'd be best to wait until tomorrow morning before you go for a bike ride, Paul."

"Ha," was all he said.

As we toured the house Bill approved of everything we'd achieved and I could sense he was sniffing out the best place for his study. Paul liked it too, he said, before skipping down the stairs and assembling his second-best titanium bike in the sparsely furnished parlour. I don't think Aunt Jean and Juan had used it much, but we planned to make it more habitable so that each couple could have their own space when desired.

By the time we sat down to supper at nine o'clock both men had settled in. Bill had requisitioned the smallest room on the second floor, overlooking the patio, and had established a makeshift study with an upright chair and a scruffy old table he'd found. His dongle worked fairly well and we saw little of him until Paul returned from his maiden bike ride, hot, sweaty and delighted. Before he could sing the praises of his route I hustled him into the bathroom and went down to help Linda put the finishing touches to our first meal together, a selection of healthy tapas and a big salad with tomatoes of a succulence I'd never tasted in England.

We felt right at home eating together as we'd done hundreds of times over the last thirty-odd years and Linda and I had agreed to propose no group activities. Rather than having a regular holiday we preferred to get into a natural rhythm right away, as if we were already living there, although we needn't have feared that the boys would propose a plethora of plans, of course. Paul's short ride had merely whetted his appetite and as he sat dreamily sipping his wine I knew he was looking forward to a longer ride the next day. Bill seemed similarly pensive, anticipating many lazy days spent reading, eating and drinking, ideally at the same time, or was he?

I caught his eye. "Bill, are you still keen on exploring the old irrigation channels that you mentioned once?"

"Yes and no, Sue, yes and no," he said, him being inordinately fond of tantalising phrases of that type.

"What do you mean?" I felt obliged to ask.

He wiped a dribble of salad dressing from his chin and grinned. "Well, in case you're thinking that the locomotive aspect of that quest is giving me cold feet, though I suppose hot feet would be more apt in this case, I assure you that isn't the case. Linda can attest to the fact that I've already begun to take brisk walks in an effort to shift some of this." He patted his belly.

She tittered. "Brisk is the word." She looked at Paul and me. "He leaves the house as if he's off to find the source of the Orinoco and within twenty minutes he's back, puffing and pulling off his new trainers."

He frowned. "Poco a poco, Linda. One mustn't overdo things."

"What does that mean?" Paul asked.

"I have to start slowly and build up my walks."

"No, the Spanish bit."

"Little by little," he said, and we never did find out why the irrigation channels were off the agenda, because we began to discuss our linguistic aspirations.

"I'm going to study for at least an hour and speak to at least one person in Spanish every day," Linda said.

"Me too," I said.

"I'll study a bit, but I'm not sure about speaking it," said Bill. "I want to get my tenses right first."

"You're sixty-five, Bill," Linda said. "By the time you get the tenses right you'll be getting a telegram from the queen, or king. There are *loads* of tenses in Spanish and every ending's different."

He grunted. "Nevertheless, I don't intend to speak like a Hollywood Indian. If I can't say a sentence right I won't say it."

"You have to be bold," said Linda. "That's what Anke told us. What about you, Paul?"

He shrugged. "Me? Oh, I'm just a tourist. I shan't be worrying about the lingo." He stretched and yawned. "Nearly time for me to hit the sack. I'll set off nice and early tomorrow and do a forty miler, I think."

"Don't get lost," I said.

"I've got maps on my phone."

"Famous last words," said Linda. "You'd better wash up now in case we never see you again."

He pushed himself up and patted his muscly thighs upon which a faint cycling sun tan line could already be seen. "Come on, Bill, duty calls."

Out on the patio Linda and I admired the geraniums, hibiscus and petunia we'd inherited and the lavender, plumbago and passion flowers which we'd bought at a nursery in Cocentaina.

Linda sipped the almond liqueur we'd both taken a liking to and looked up at the stars. "Well, this *is* nice."

I inhaled the heady mixed aroma. "Yes, it is."

"What are we going to do tomorrow, Sue?"

"I don't know. I thought we weren't making plans."

"Yes, I know, but we need some sort of objective, however small."

"We'll need some bread. We can go to the bakery. Anke says they don't speak English there."

Her eyes opened wide. "Ooh, yes, and we'll talk to them for as long as we can. I can't wait."

"Right, so is that a good enough plan for you?"

"Oh, yes, we don't want to overdo it. We'll save the grocer's for another day."

I chuckled. "Linda, anyone hearing this conversation might think we were two sad middle-aged ladies."

She bristled comically. "Us? Get away! Anyway, we'll be going to the pool later on. That's bound to be memorable even if the bakery isn't."

That and something else Linda had said made me later believe that she might have become somewhat prophetic.

The trip to the bakery was a great success. A stout lady of about our age called Lola was very welcoming and immediately began to speak about Aunt Jean, elongating her name rather than shortening it as the man at the hotel had done. I was understandably nonplussed by her rapid monologue, but Linda smiled brazenly, nodded and chipped in with a 'sí' or 'no' when she felt it appropriate. Only when Lola ended a sentence with an interrogatory intonation and an enquiring smile did my sister's confident expression falter slightly.

"Get out of that one, clever clogs," I murmured.

She cleared her throat. "Lola, puedes repetir la pregunta, por favor?" she said, before flashing me an exultant glance.

Lola repeated the question and we divined that she was asking if we were settling in all right.

"Sí, muy bien, gracias," said Linda, which I topped with, "El pueblo es muy bonito y agradable," before she followed up with that old chestnut, "Hoy es soleado y hace calor."

"*Mucho* calor," I said, fanning my face.

Linda then correctly asked for two long baguettes and after cheery goodbyes we left while the going was good.

"She'll tell everyone we're fluent now," Linda said as she strode majestically along the cobbled street.

"Hola, buenos días," I chirped when an elderly lady walked by.

"Bon día," she replied with a smile.

"That's Valenciano," said Linda.

"I know."

"Once we've perfected our Spanish we'll make short work of that."

"Piece of cake," I said, and we burst out laughing, before rushing into the house lest they take us for lunatics.

Bill looked up from his musty old book. "What are you two so cheerful about?"

Linda frowned and waved a finger. "Solo español, por favor, Señor Bill."

He flicked up his glasses and shook a finger. "Ha, no, you only say señor with the surname."

"Never mind. No importa. Say something in Spanish, you coward."

He glanced at a notebook on the arm of the chair and began to recite something that sounded ominously historical.

"Vamos, Sue. Let's get out of here."

When we'd calmed down we made a pot of tea, took Bill a cup, and repaired to the shaded patio to dutifully fulfil our hour's study for the day. After ten minutes of boring verbs Linda asked me when Paul was due back.

"Er, he set off at seven, so about half an hour ago, I'd say."

"Must have gone a bit further then."

"Yes, he's got his phone, so there's no need to worry."

When the hour was up I'd begun to worry.

"Call him then."

"He won't like that. He'll say I'm making a fuss."

Nevertheless I called him a short time later.

"Hello, Sue."

"Hi, we were just wondering where you'd got to."

"I'm just taking a short break now, but I'll be off soon and home within the hour."

"OK. Are you in a bar?"

"Something like that. See you in a bit."

I hung up and pursed my lips.

"What's up?" Linda asked.

"Oh, nothing. It sounded very quiet where he is. I could tell he was inside, but it was too quiet for a bar, especially a Spanish one."

She tutted and shook her head. "Oh, don't tell me he's got a fancy woman already?"

"Looks like it. She must be a titanium push-biker's moll."

"Don't worry, we'll find ourselves a bit on the side this aft at the pool."

In the event Paul's explanation sounded so far-fetched that over lunch the three of us quizzed him very thoroughly, especially Bill, who loves a bit of intrigue.

He dipped a length of carrot in the low-calorie mayonnaise and waved it about. "So, to recap, you went further than you meant to and ended up near Finestrat."

"Yes."

"I told you he'd get lost," said Linda.

"I didn't get lost, it was just that the road I chose took me nearer to the coast than I'd meant to go. I was right above Benidorm, but I managed to get past it towards La Nucia and take another road back over the mountains. It was bloody busy up there and it turned out they were all going to this place called Guadalest. The bars were full of tourists, so I pressed on past a reservoir and that's when I bonked."

We were all familiar with the cycling verb 'to bonk', which means to run out of energy and begin to feel light-headed.

"And that's when you met this chap, is it?" Bill asked.

"Yes, he caught me up."

"Were you bonked by the roadside or bonking on the bike?" said Linda with an admirably straight face.

"I was plodding on. I had no food and only a bit of water, so I just wanted to get to the top and grab something somewhere down the other side. Anyway, he comes alongside on this top of the range Colnago bike – carbon, of course, but a beautiful piece of kit – and seeing the state I was in he gave me a gel and an energy bar. I was fine after I'd had them. I wasn't knackered, you see, just out of fuel."

"Of course," I said loyally.

"Anyway, we passed a nice village called Confrides and coming down the other side he told me he had a little place near Gorga, so I ended up going there for a proper bite to eat." He shrugged. "He was a bit insistent and it would have been rude to refuse."

Bill stabbed a strip of pepper and lay down his fork. "Right, so, up to this point it all sounds perfectly believable, Paul, but don't you think you've let your imagination run riot with what follows?"

"You might have still been bonking without realising it," said Linda. "Having hallucinations."

Paul shrugged. "I don't care if you believe me or not. Pass me a bit of chicken, love."

After that he refused to be drawn out, so we only had his initial version of events. His saviour was a lean, tanned man of about fifty called Arthur and his 'little place' turned out to be a huge chalet tucked away almost out of sight of the road down a narrow but perfectly asphalted track. The light-blue house was enclosed within high white walls and when they reached the large gate a youngish, muscly man in mirrored sunglasses appeared from nowhere and opened the gates using a hand-held device. This man, Arthur said, was one of the three security guards he employed, and between them they worked a twenty-four hour rota when he was residing there. As they pushed their bikes up the short drive the guard – an ex-SAS man, Arthur said – trotted ahead and opened the front door, which Paul swore was about six inches thick. Arthur assured Paul that his bike would be safe outside, before wheeling his own into a windowless room full of vintage and modern pushbikes that made Paul's mouth water. Arthur estimated their total market value at £60,000, give or take a few thousand, and Paul duly expressed his admiration, upon which he said that collecting them was his little hobby.

From there they entered a modern sitting room where a few light bites had already been laid out, along with a large carafe of iced water, as Arthur said he never drank anything else. While they snacked Paul commented on the extent of his security arrangements, to which he replied that when the council told him to take the rolls of razor wire off the tops of the walls, he had little choice but to employ two more 'handy chaps' to look after his little place. Paul said Arthur's accent was the sort that used to be heard a lot on the BBC; so posh, in fact, that he believed he might be a closet foreigner. Before escorting Paul outside he showed him another little room which contained, to his and our surprise, several bulletproof vests and sundry stun guns, as one never knew what sort of miscreants might put in an appearance when one least expected them. When the ex-SAS man appeared from nowhere and opened the gate, Arthur said he would like to ride with Paul again, as despite having owned the house for six years and cycled many thousands of miles around the area he had yet to find a suitable cycling companion. Paul mentioned cycling clubs but he replied that he preferred to ride alone or with one congenial companion, as he wasn't a gregarious person and also feared crashes when riding in a group.

When Paul had clamped up we'd still had lots of questions to ask him, but he later confessed to me that he knew little more about the enigmatic cyclist. He'd said that he lived alone and divided his time between his Spanish retreat, his apartment in London and his little 'bolthole' in Marrakesh. Paul had noticed no family photos in the house. He showed me a plain card on which was handwritten only his first name and a Spanish mobile number.

"So will you call him?" I asked as we were getting our swimming things together.

"Yes, I think so. He's a decent rider and he's not far away, so we might as well meet up and go for a spin one day."

"Don't you find him intriguing?"

He shrugged. "He's just another cyclist to me. When I meet up with someone on the road we don't tell each other our life stories."

I squeezed his arm. "You must be a *bit* intrigued though, admit it."

He smiled. "Yeah, well, we'll see what I find out if we go for a ride."

When we arrived at the pool at about half past three it was practically empty, but little by little people began to arrive and by five there must have been forty of us within the fenced compound, a few on the red plastic chairs near the tiny bar and most on the patchy grass around the decent-sized pool, complete with a handsome young lifeguard. The pool is set slightly outside the village and has great views up and down the hillside, so I had to agree with Anke that it was a splendid amenity for such a small place. We set up camp with our towels and parasol as far as possible from the bar, as the techno music that the portly, red-faced, middle-aged man in charge seemed to like wasn't our cup of tea at all. Most of the teenagers hung around there, while families, young couples and half a dozen wrinkly foreigners opted for the grass.

Paul had a quick swim, lay down and fell promptly asleep, as he'd cycled fifty-odd miles that morning in addition to all the excitement at his friend Arthur's little place.

Linda poked her slumbering husband's arm with her foot. "Bill, me and Sue have talked Spanish and studied for an hour today."

"Jolly good," he mumbled.

"What about you?" She winked at me. "What have you achieved, linguistically speaking?"

"I was about to tell you this morning when you ran away."

"Sorry, love, what was it?"

He sat up and clasped his hands around his knees. "Well, I translated a paragraph from a Spanish history book I picked up back home into English, then back into Spanish again."

"Er, isn't that cheating, Bill?" I said.

"How so, Sue?"

"I mean, if you had the book there in front of you it can't have been much of a challenge."

"Ah, yes, but I closed it. I wanted to see how similar it would end up, you see." His smiling face clouded somewhat.

"And?"

"Hmm, well, it wasn't. In fact it was gobbledegook, apart from the blanks."

Linda snorted daintily. "Don't be a chump, Bill. That sort of thing's far too hard. You need to start with the basics. Look, why don't you go and get us a drink and start chatting to someone over there?"

"All right, I will." He pushed himself up and walked towards the bar, before returning for his wallet and setting off again with a resolute look on his face.

From our vantage point on the slightly sloping grass bank we saw him engage with the red-faced barman and a conversation with much gesticulation ensued.

"He must be trying to speak Spanish or he'd never wave his arms around like that," Linda murmured.

"And that chap doesn't look the type who'd speak much English," I observed.

"I can't see any drinks yet."

"What on earth can Bill be saying to him?"

"God knows. Oh, he's finally getting the drinks. I must say he's done pretty well to talk for so long. I reckon he's matched our effort in the bakery."

Bill then loped around the pool with two cans of coke.

"You've forgotten yours," I said.

He shook his head, smiled and hurried back to the bar, where he and the man sat down in the shade and continued to talk. When Paul awoke some time later they were still gabbing away and we'd concluded that they couldn't possibly have been speaking Spanish for so long.

I pointed across the pool. "Bill's made a friend."

"Go and get yourself a drink, Paul," said Linda. "Try to sneak up on them and see what they're chattering about."

He yawned. "Bound to be history or something."

"That chap doesn't look much like a historian to me," I said.

"No, more like a lush," said Linda. "He can't have got so red just from the sun, not to mention all those broken veins on that great big nose of his. I think they'll be talking about, er… oh, about us being here. What do you think, Sue?"

"Hmm, it seems too intense for that. I'll have to go with history. Paul?"

"What?"

"What do you think they're talking about?"

He got up and stretched his legs. "All the women they've slept with. I'll go and see." He walked ten paces, returned for his wallet, and set off again.

"Dozy sods."

"I think they both forgot them because it feels so relaxed here," I said. "I reckon most people know each other. I saw one man serve himself while they were nattering."

Paul returned presently with a can of beer.

"Well?"

"Machu Picchu."

"We've been there," said Linda.

"Well it seems the chap has too."

Her tanned face appeared to pale slightly. "They're not speaking... Spanish, are they?"

"Course not, or how would I have known what they were on about? The bloke speaks pretty good English, or American."

Linda flopped back onto her towel and sighed. "Thank God for that."

Five minutes later she decided she was thirsty after all and made for the bar. After a while, as the music emanating from the speakers had become more pleasant, Paul and I collected our stuff and walked over. Bill's new friend soon joined us at our rickety table.

"Hiya, I'm Alberto," he said, before kissing me and pumping Paul's hand. He smelt of beer and slightly of sweat, but it was a hot day and he'd been too busy talking to take a dip.

"Alberto's travelled a lot," said Bill. "Proper travelling, spending time in places and meeting people."

Alberto's beaming face and glittering if rather bloodshot brown eyes made me fear that we might be in for a long travel monologue, but instead he asked us what we thought of the village so far. I told him we loved it and Linda asked him if he lived there.

"Nope, me and my wife live in Cocentaina, right over there. I run this lil place every summer and try to get away from here in the fall."

"Tell them about Cambodia, Alberto."

He shrugged. "Had to be careful with the goddam landmines when I was there, but the folks were friendly." He nodded and sipped his beer.

"Does your wife travel with you?" the nosey one asked.

"No, ma'am, she ain't into travelling. Besides, she works all year. Excuse me, guys, I'd better go and serve those kids."

He didn't return to our table, instead remaining behind the scruffy bar and chatting to some local youngsters in what we suspected was Valenciano, as we caught scarcely a word.

"How come he talked to you so much?" Linda asked.

Bill shrugged. "He recognised a kindred spirit, I guess."

"I *guess*? You never say I guess."

"I guess I've picked it up from Alberto then. He lived in the States for a few years when he was younger."

"So he travels while his wife works, does he?" Linda muttered.

He grinned. "Some guys' wives know their place."

"Unlike yours," she said.

"Unlike mine, yes. Ah, one of my few regrets is that I haven't travelled as much as I'd have liked."

"But you've been all over the place," I said. "Iceland, Thailand, Japan, New Zealand."

"And Peru." He sighed. "Yes, but I mean really travel, like Alberto did. He just packed his rucksack and set off for weeks on end."

"Did you say did?"

"Well, from what I can gather he's on a tighter leash these days. I think his selfish wife has got fed up of him spending all their money and he hasn't been abroad for a while."

"Spending all *her* money," Linda said.

"She's happier here with her family."

"Is that what he told you?"

"No, but that's the impression I got."

"Do they have children?" I asked.

"Sue, I've only just met the man. No doubt I'll find out another day."

Linda sighed sonorously. "Damn it, Sue. Paul's got his mysterious cycling buddy and this one's got his roving traveller."

"I know, and we've only got Lola at the bakery."

"Still, we haven't been to the grocer's yet. Who knows what thrills are awaiting us there? Oh, and we've got Anke too, if she counts."

"Why shouldn't she count?" I said.

"Oh, I don't know. She sort of took us under her wing when we first came out and seems to know everything that's going on. She speaks Spanish too well for us to knock about with her much. I mean, I like her, of course, but she isn't the same sort of catch as the ones these two have made."

"She must be an alpha female and these two are betas," Bill said to Paul.

"I reckon so. They think she'll cramp their style."

"Does your cycling friend speak Spanish?" I asked Paul.

"Dunno, probably. He seems pretty sharp."

"Are you going to call him soon?" Linda asked.

"In a few days. Don't want him thinking I'm *so* impressed with his setup."

Linda stood up and pulled on a flimsy, colourful dress that she'd found in Aunt Jean's wardrobe. "I'm off. I want to have a proper shower at home."

We all prepared to leave except Bill.

"I guess I'll just stick around for a while," he said.

Sure enough, before we'd passed through the gates Alberto was by his side with two fresh beers.

# 6

The grocer's was a disappointment. The lady on the till carried on chatting to a friend while she beeped through our modest purchase, so hearty greetings and a brief comment about the heat were all that we managed. We stopped off for a drink on the way home and sat at a table while the local men propped up the bar.

"It's harder to chat to folk if you're a woman," I murmured.

"And being together speaking English doesn't help."

"So if you were alone would you be up at the bar?"

She nibbled her bottom lip. "Hmm, yes, I might. I mean, the other bar is a real noisy blokes place, but they seem more civilised here. Yes, I think I'd take a pew up there, just for a quick coffee."

"They might think you're a hussy."

She flicked back her hair and pouted. "Yeah, well, I know how to fend off the wrong sort of chap."

"I'll let you come alone next time then."

She shrugged. "I suppose it would be good not to go around like Siamese twins all the time. Paul and Bill have met their buddies by going it alone."

"True. Still, we've only just arrived and we'll be leaving in a fortnight."

"I wish we were staying for longer."

"Me too, but you two can if you want."

"No, those flights were dear and the grass'll be six inches long as it is. We could come back in autumn when it's a bit cheaper."

I sighed. "Yes, I think Paul should be able to get a week off. I wonder if he's going to go cycling every morning."

She tittered. "Let him get his fill. Fingers crossed the weather will be rubbish when we get back."

"Why?"

"Well, he'll drive to work and back in the rain. Then he'll probably do that daft cycling he does in the garage and think about how great life would be here."

"Hmm, he might."

"Paul's the missing link, Sue."

I chuckled. "That's not a very nice thing to say, Sue. I know he's taciturn, but he's just as bright as Bill in his way."

"But you know what I mean."

"Yes, that once he retires we can all come here whenever we like."

"Work on him, Sue."

I tutted. "Paul doesn't respond to that sort of stimulus. He needs to make his own mind up about things."

"I dare say you're right. Come on, Bill needs this tuna for the lunch he's making us."

"Tuna salad?"

"What else?"

At the pool Bill chatted to Alberto, Paul snoozed, and Linda and I worked on our prepositions. On arriving home at about half past seven I decided to take a leaf out of Linda's theoretical book and slipped out of the house alone. I wandered down towards the park and found quite a few people ambling around, so I slackened my pace and greeted everyone I met. The park isn't long enough to stroll up and down too many times, so I perched on a bench and smiled vacantly as I watched the sun setting over the hills. A young couple with a small boy commented on the agreeable breeze and two elderly ladies asked me if we were settling in all right.

"Yes, but now only holiday," I said in Spanish. "In autumn we come for more time."

"Bien, bien," one said, while the other nodded approvingly.

A few youths appeared with some bottles of beer, but they weren't wearing hoods and they too said hola as they passed, so I walked contentedly home.

"Where have you been?" Linda asked.

"Out making my own friends."

"And?"

"I'm booked up for lunch and dinner for the rest of our stay."

"Ha."

"No, but you were right. They pay you more attention if you're alone, but what the heck. Once we're here for longer we'll meet everyone eventually."

"Yes, let's chill out and go with the flow."

"And maybe go to the beach one day."

"If the boys can spare the time."

During the next few days we got into a pleasant routine and Linda and I stopped fretting about meeting people. Paul cycled, ate and dozed by the pool, while Bill took short walks, read, ate and talked to Alberto. Linda and I pottered around the house and village and later swam, sunbathed and studied. We all took a stroll in the evenings and dined at home or in the bar. On the second Monday we drove down to Villajoyosa and spent a couple of hours on the hot, crowded beach, before eating a mediocre seafood paella and driving back to the relative peace of the pool.

"It's nice to spend time by the sea, but there are too many damn tourists at this time of year," said Paul.

I smiled. "I thought you said you were just a tourist too?"

"Yeah, well, not that kind of tourist."

"The beach'll be better in late September and October," Linda said. Paul spotted her customary wink so she rubbed her eye.

"It'll be better for cycling then too," he said. "By ten o'clock it's getting a bit too hot to be out on the bike, especially if you're climbing."

"Will you be able to get a week or so off in the autumn?" Linda asked him.

"I can take time off whenever I want," he said rather brusquely. "It is my company after all, or part of it. It'll be time for me to work a bit less soon anyway."

Bill's mouth opened, but my eyes indicated that he oughtn't to say more.

"I'm out for a ride with Arthur tomorrow."

"Ooh, will he invite you to his fortress again?" said Linda.

He shrugged. "No reason why he should. We're meeting in Gorga and I think we'll come back this way, so it'll be my turn to invite him."

"We'll make sure we're in then," Linda said. "I'm dying to meet him."

Bill clicked his tongue. "I bet he won't come. Sounds like a born loner to me. I know the type well."

Linda laughed. "You know lots of rich folk with security guards, do you?"

"Ten euros says he won't come."

"You're on." She wrinkled her nose and frowned. "Hang on, I don't think he'll come either."

"Too late now, love."

Bill won the bet because Arthur declined Paul's offer of a drink and continued homeward.

Paul wheeled his bike into the house, sweating from every pore. "He's a strong bugger, but he is five years younger than me."

I whipped one of his t-shirts from the washing machine and handed it to him. "Did he tell you anything else about himself?"

He wiped his face, neck, arms and legs. "God, that last little climb was hot work. Oh, he told me he does something in the City but works mostly online. He got divorced twelve years ago and says he hasn't bothered much with women since then. He's got a son who works in finance too, but he doesn't see much of him. That's about it. We were going too fast to talk much."

Linda breezed in. "Well, what did the cycling Croesus have to say?"

"Sue'll fill you in. I'm off for a shower."

"You're all red. You'll get heatstroke cycling in this sun."

"Yeah, we're going out an hour earlier on Friday." He tossed the t-shirt back into the washer and tramped slowly up the stairs.

"I reckon it'll be perfect for cycling here, except in July and August," Linda murmured. "All winter long he'd be like a pig in you-know-what. Shall I point that out to him?"

"No, Linda, leave him be. I think his mental processes are working just the way you want them to."

"*We* want them to."

"Yes."


Bill and his pal chatted for at least an hour every single afternoon, as Alberto worked seven days a week for almost four months. This was why he needed eight months to recover from his summer stint, Bill claimed one evening in the park.

"What rot," Linda said.

"How long has he been living this life of Riley?" I asked.

"Oh, about fifteen years, I think. He was in Philadelphia and then Atlanta for a few years in his twenties, then when he came back he got married and opened a photography shop in Alcoy. That lasted for a few years before he got bored of it – the shop, not the wife – and then he got the pool job, so he was free to travel in winter."

"Some guys have all the luck," said Paul.

"Any kids?" I asked.

"No."

"But you said that he's not travelling much now," I said.

Bill smiled. "He's not travelling *abroad* much. He always gets a couple of good trips in around Spain." He coughed lightly. "In fact I might, er… shoot off with him for a week or two this winter."

"Whoa! Stop right there," Linda cried. "We don't even know how long we'll be here yet and you're already planning to desert me."

Bill looked suitably sheepish. "It's just an idea. I didn't promise anything." He glanced at Paul. "If we don't end up coming for long I shan't go away with him."

Paul put a sandalled foot on the edge of a bench and breathed in the fragrant air. "If it's me you're worried about, then don't. I think I'll start to train up a lad we've got and I reckon in two or three months I'll become a consultant."

"Can you do that?" said Linda.

"What does that entail?" I said at the same time.

"Yes, I can, because another partner who officially retired a couple of years ago does it. It'll entail going in for a week or so every couple of months and doing some work online the rest of the time. I'll put it to them when we get back." He looked at Linda. "Satisfied?"

She feigned surprise. "Me, Paul? I'm not your missus. Ask her."

I took his arm. "Do what you think is best, love."

"This calls for a bottle of cava to celebrate," said Bill, accelerating away towards the bar.

Our remaining days passed quickly and no longer felt like a mere holiday, as we were all making plans for the autumn. We shared some of them with Anke and Rik when they came to dinner. They'd enjoyed their trip to Asturias and part of Galicia and Rik swore that his next job would be his last.

"I'm going to Nigeria soon. I hate it there, so it's a good job to finish with."

"He's said that before," Anke said.

"Yes, but as we will soon have these new delighting (sic) neighbours, I mean it this time."

We chuckled and cooed accordingly. Paul got on well with Rik, I was glad to see, while Bill remained strangely aloof. When Rik mentioned his passion for photography I said that Alberto at the pool had once owned a shop and was still an aficionado, according to the man who then frowned at me, evidently not keen to share his pal with another foreigner. He needn't have worried.

Rik laughed deeply. "Oh, that Alberto is a lazy, drunken devil. All day long drinking beer and talking when he should be keeping the place tidy and the water clean."

"Isn't it clean?" Linda asked.

"It could be cleaner, and clearer. I have no time for that man, and oh, the music he plays to please his young customers. In my opinion he lacks dignity and the working ethics."

Bill's face remained impassive, but I pictured him making an invisible sign of the cross over Rik. At that moment I'd have sworn they would never hit it off, but life is a long and winding road and... well, you'll see in due course.

"So, Paul, please tell us about your plans for work that Sue mentioned," said Anke.

He told her briefly.

"Oh, that is so good! Soon all four of you will be living here all the time."

"We haven't decided that yet," I said. "We like our homes in England too and, well, there are lots of things to think about."

"Your children, you mean?"

"No," said Paul. "They have their own lives and they can come out whenever they like, if we're here, that is."

Linda sighed. "Our Luke will get an invite too, but not whenever he likes, as he's capable of getting his feet too firmly under the table."

"What's that?" Rik asked.

Bill patted the table, then his legs. "Like we are now, except for weeks and weeks, but it's not going to happen."

"Where is he now?" I asked.

"In Derbyshire, I think, doing some building work with a friend, unless you've heard any different, Linda?"

"He mentioned going to France to do some kayaking courses," she said.

"Since when is he a kayak instructor?" Paul asked.

"Since he got a certificate, or so he says." Bill sighed and shook his head. "He must have got his wanderlust from me."

Linda chuckled.

"France is next to Spain," I pointed out.

"He'll be here sooner or later, I fear," his loving father said. "Anyway, never mind Luke. As soon as we get back here I'm going to order some office furniture for our study."

I raised my brows. "Will it be *our* study, Bill?"

"Of course, I'm not going to requisition a whole room to myself, am I? If we all did that we'd soon run out of space."

"I can shove my bikes in one of the empty rooms," said Paul.

"Bikes?" Linda said.

"Yes, I can't make do with just one when I'm here for longer."

"But you can only ride one at once."

He sighed. "Yes, Linda, but when it rains I'll need one with mudguards, won't I?"

"Not here," said Rik. "Here when it rains it rains so hard that you won't wish to go out, but it only lasts a few days."

"We'll see."

"We'll have a few weeks to make arrangements," I said, wondering how radical those arrangements would be.

Only two more noteworthy things happened before we flew home, the first being a communication breakdown at the grocer's. Linda had allowed me to go and I was delighted to see the lady alone at the till, so I grabbed a couple of things and remarked that the sky was a bit cloudy. She agreed that it was, before launching into a high-speed monologue of which I caught hardly a word. I raised a hand and asked her to speak more slowly, and although she slowed down slightly I still hadn't the foggiest idea of what she was talking about. Blushing and nodding like an idiot, I took my change, said goodbye and staggered out into the street.

"I wouldn't worry about it," Linda said as she handed me a cup of tea.

"Oh, you might have done better, but she lost me completely and just went on and on. I had no… context to get a grip on. I wonder if she did it on purpose."

"I doubt it. I think she went to Aunt Jean's funeral. Maybe she thought you'd speak as well as she did. You do look a bit like her."

"Why don't you go and buy something and see if she does the same to you?"

"Don't be daft, Sue. Look, we'll get down to some serious studying when we get home."

"And listening practice, lots of listening practice. We need to be better prepared next time," I said, later reflecting that my debacle had been a timely reminder that our Spanish was still rudimentary to say the least.

The second event of note was the arrival of the English couple and their guests. During the early hours of our second-to-last night we heard faint music from outside the village, so Bill took his morning stroll in that direction and duly reported back to base.

"There's a dusty Range Rover with British plates and a cleanish BMW with Spanish plates. From that I deduce that the Range Rover has been driven some distance, probably from England, and the BMW has been hired, possibly at the airport."

"Good work, Sherlock," said Linda. "What else did you spot?"

He stroked his chin and frowned comically. "The disorderly state of the pool furniture they've taken outside since their arrival suggests they made use of it last night while imbibing large quantities of alcoholic beverages, evidence of which was still present."

"But is the pool clean?" I asked.

"It's been clean for at least a week, since I last took the sewage works route."

"They must have a man," said Linda.

"We don't need a man." I said. "We'll just lock the doors and ask Anke to keep an eye on it."

"Did you see them?" Linda asked Bill.

"No, but I heard one of them speaking in an unmistakable regional accent."

Linda grinned. "It must be cockney. English gangsters are always cockneys."

"No, try again."

"North or south?" I asked.

"North."

"Geordies?"

"North-west."

"Lancashire?" Linda said.

"Hmm, close. They're by the sea, more or less."

"Scousers!"

"Correct."

"Oh, that's all right then. I like Liverpool folk."

"Do you know any?" I asked.

"Well, not personally, but I used to watch Brookside. I liked a lot of the characters in that, though that Barry Grant was a bad 'un."

"They were actors, love."

"I *know* that, Bill. I wonder if they'll go to the pool. I'd like to meet them."

"They've got their own pool," I said, not being especially keen to meet them.

Just then Paul returned from his final bike ride. By then he had a little towel by the door so as not to sully the tiles with his sweat. He left his bike in the hallway and clip-clopped in.

"Ah, I enjoyed that." He prodded his little bike computer. "That makes 563 miles altogether and..." More prodding. "...oh, I'll check the total feet of climbing when I upload it." He patted his thighs and smiled. "I'll give them hell when I get back, especially on the climbs."

I tapped my phone. "The forecast is sixteen degrees and showers."

"Oh, well, it'll make a change."

"The Scouse gangsters are here," Linda said.

"What? Who?"

"The English people who we know nothing whatsoever about, except that they might be from Liverpool, have arrived with some friends, but as we're off tomorrow morning I doubt we'll see them," I said rather prudishly.

"I wonder what sort of guns they've got," said Linda, just to wind me up.

"Hmm, the law is very strict about handguns here," said Bill. "Although plenty of folk in the country have shotguns, I believe."

"Has your chum got one?" Linda asked.

"Three, all licensed. He'll probably take me hunting in winter."

"Anything you shoot you'll have to skin and cook," I said. "That's the only way you can justify killing defenceless creatures."

"Shame we won't see the gangsters this time," Linda murmured.

That evening we saw five people from the Liverpool area sitting at table outside the bar, dressed as if at the seaside. I suggesting going inside, but by way of reply Linda sat down at another table with a party of locals between us and them. We joined her and the friendly young waiter came out to take our order.

"Let's have a jug of sangria like them," Linda said. "We haven't had one yet and it'll give us some common ground." She smiled at the lad. "Una jarra de sangría, por favor, Fran."

"Enseguida, Linda." He trotted off.

"Right, let's just try to tune in and find out what they're talking about," Linda murmured.

"It's our last night, Linda," I grumbled. "I'd hoped to reflect on the time we've spent here, not eavesdrop on a load of rough-looking folk."

She narrowed her eyes. "But we need to know who we're dealing with, Sue."

"Stop being silly," Bill said quite sternly.

Paul sighed, stood up and walked over to their table. He introduced himself, hands were shaken, a jovial conversation took place and he returned about three minutes later.

"Well?" Linda mouthed.

Luckily the locals were talking quite loudly by then, so as Paul had his back to them he was able to fill us in without whispering. "Wayne and Kerry own the house and the other couple and the old bloke are friends from home. They're here for a fortnight and usually come out four or five times a year, Wayne said."

"Who's Wayne?" Linda asked.

"He's the big bloke with the goatee and the tattooed arms. Kerry's the big woman next to him. I've forgotten the names of the others."

"What do they do?" Linda asked.

"Well, I mentioned I was about to retire from engineering and the old bloke just said they worked the markets, so I assume that meant all of them."

"Ooh, that could mean anything," said Linda. "Money markets, fish markets, *arms* markets."

"Drugs markets, extortion markets" I added, in case she thought they were just jolly Robin Hood type crooks who wouldn't harm a fly.

Paul sighed. "I think he meant market markets, as in market stalls of some kind."

"They must pay well," Bill said.

"And why not, if they have a few? Look, they seemed OK to me and all we want is to get along with them."

I emptied my glass and refilled it. "Can we talk about something else now, please?"

"She's annoyed," Linda murmured, sticking out her lower lip, something she'd done to annoy me since we were about eight and six respectively.

"I just want to go home with memories of all the nice people we've met." All eyes were upon me. "We don't associate with people like them at home, do we? We don't hang out in rough pubs to meet folk from the seedier side of life, do we?" I said, mostly to Linda. I drained my glass. "I'm going home to relax on the patio. I'll see you back there."

I stood up just as the party in question got to their feet and when Wayne and Kerry came over I was wearing my most beguiling smile. I greeted them and ended up introducing them to Bill and Linda.

"We knew your aunt," Kerry said.

I tore my eyes away from the tasteful Liverpool F.C. tattoo just above her cleavage. "Oh, really?"

"Yes, we're sorry for your loss."

"Thank you. Yes, we've been hoping to meet people who knew her."

"We've had the house for about ten years, you see, and she used to walk a lot then, sometimes with her sketchbook. She often popped in for a drink and we called in on her too. She gave us a lovely painting of the village. I wanted to pay her for it but she wouldn't have it. It's the first thing we see when we go into the lounge, isn't it, Wayne?"

"Yeah, I like it a lot. We didn't see so much of her these last few years. I think she was looking after Juan most of the time and we didn't like to disturb them. It was a shock when we came and found out she'd just died. We missed the funeral by a day too, worse luck."

"Oh, that's a shame," I gushed. "Would you like to sit down?"

"No, ta. We'd better get back. We were up late last night. What with all the excitement of getting here we had a few too many. You'll have to come round sometime."

I nodded eagerly. "Oh, yes, thanks, we will, when we get back. We're off tomorrow, you see."

Kerry sighed with apparent sincerity. "What a shame. We'll be out again in a few weeks, I think."

"Oh, we might be here then too. Bill here is a great walker, so he can call in and we can arrange to meet up."

"Great," said Wayne. "We'll be off then. Cheerio for now."

I remained standing until they'd gone around the corner, then sat down in a dignified manner and carefully smoothed my colourful skirt, one of Aunt Jean's nifty numbers.

"I told you Scousers were the salt of the earth," Linda said, but to be fair she refrained from teasing me about my chameleon-like transformation. We stayed on to drink a second jug of sangria and talked about other things.

Later in bed I said Kerry and Wayne were probably all right really.

Paul stroked my arm and yawned. "Yeah, they're not as classy as what I am, but they're friendly enough."

"That sounds more Welsh than Scouse."

"Oh, well. G'night, love."

I guessed that Linda would still be speculating about the nature of their profession and Bill would be begging her to let him sleep. I asked him in the morning and it turned out I'd guessed right.

On the flight back each couple had adjacent window and middle seats and we spent the first part of the journey looking at the views.

"Who knows?" said Bill. "Me and Alberto might be down there somewhere in those hills this autumn, hiking along and camping out in the open without a care in the world."

"We'll see about that," said Linda. "I haven't vetted him properly yet. If Rik's right and he's a boozehound I'm not letting you out of my sight with him."

"Oh, he's not a boozehood at all. He just likes sipping beer."

"All day long."

"No, he drinks coffee too..."

"It looks like good cycling country all over Spain," Paul said to me.

"But you're not keen on cycle touring."

"Not with loads of bags, no, but we could shoot off somewhere and I'd take the bike along." He glanced at my profile. "Maybe."

I smiled, remembering how he'd generously agreed to drastically cut down his workload. Paul had always enjoyed the challenges of his job and loved being a co-owner, but he'd perceived that he was the missing link and would now take steps to fall into line with the rest of us.

"Yes, you could do that," I said. "There's a whole new country down there for us to explore."

"With tons of fascinating historical sites," said an eavesdropping Bill.

Linda's eyes appeared over her seat. "It's going to be brilliant."

"Yes, I think it is."

# 7

Unaccustomed as we were to having so much time on our hands, Linda and I met up every morning to study Spanish. Mornings were best, she said, because our brains would be at their freshest, so we spent at least an hour working intensively on our grammar, before 'chatting' for a while and finally finding something Spanish to watch on YouTube. We preferred documentaries because the film gave us a good idea of what they were talking about and we usually found a fairly clear bit and played it back over and over again until we understood as much as we could.

During one especially strenuous repeat-listening session Bill arrived back from his walk and trotted straight up the stairs.

Linda pressed pause and chuckled. "Do you know what he'll be doing now?"

I heard more footsteps on the stairs. "Whatever it was he was quick about it."

"He'll have weighed himself. He weighs himself after every walk, twice a day."

"Twice?"

"Oh, yes, he's as serious about losing weight as we are about learning Spanish."

"Morning, Sue."

"Hi, Bill."

"I'm under eighty-five."

"I know," I said, perplexed.

"He means kilos. Well done, love."

He shrugged and patted his slightly reduced paunch. "It's all about willpower. I was ninety-one last winter, eighty-nine before Spain, eighty-seven after Spain and eighty-four-point-nine now. I aim to get down to eighty before we go back. Me and Alberto are going to do some long walks."

"Is he on a diet too?" I asked.

"Not yet. He says it's hard to lose weight at the pool because of all the free beer. When he has to pay for it he drinks much less, he says."

Linda snorted.

"Did you and Alberto ever speak Spanish together?" I asked.

He frowned. "Hmm, that's something I wish to address when we go back. In fact I wrote him an email in Spanish the other day, with a little help from a translating tool."

Another snort. "A lot of help."

"And he wrote back in English, so I don't think he's got the message yet. He enjoys speaking American, you see, but he has to realise that if I'm going to be living there he'll have to speak Spanish to me at least some of the time."

"You should study with us."

He wrinkled his nose. "Hmm, thanks, but I'd rather go it alone. I'm studying the pluscuamperfecto tense now and it's tricky stuff."

"I haven't heard of that one."

"It's just the past perfect," said Linda. "Bill, listen to this." She played the snippet of the travel documentary we'd been listening to.

He frowned and nodded slowly.

She paused it. "Did you get that?"

"Er, not a dicky bird. Oh, hang on, Praga is Prague, isn't it?"

She smiled complacently. "Well done. Me and Sue understood most of that, eventually. If you don't do some listening practice, all the pluscuamperfectos in the world aren't going to help you have a conversation."

"How's Paul's Spanish coming along?" he asked me.

"He..."

"Never mind Paul," Linda said. "We're talking about you."

He shrugged. "I prefer to do things my own way. I'm more academically minded than you."

"Paul isn't doing much," I said. "He's really busy at work now and he thinks he's too old to learn it anyway."

"What rot," said Linda. "Still, if he's busy I won't harass him about it until we're out there. I'll make some tea."

As we'd only just finished a cup I guessed she had something significant to say, as Linda often broaches crucial subjects while pouring from the pot.

"Bill and I have been thinking," she said as she poured. "We might rent this house out. Milk?"

"Yes," I said, having taken milk in my tea for the last fifty years.

"Which would mean us living in the house in Spain. Half a sugar?"

"Yes, as usual. That's fine by me, Linda. The house is yours just as much as mine. Oh, I mentioned putting the house in both our names to Paul and he said to hang fire."

"Oh?"

I stirred my tea thoroughly, having some news of my own to impart. "Yes, he said to wait because he thinks that in the long term we might want to have a house each over there."

Bill grinned. "Four houses?"

"Just two, I think, to begin with, anyway, but not until we've spent ages there. So, if we buy another house or you buy another house or we both decide to buy other houses it makes sense to leave the house in my name for now, as it won't be cheap to get it changed."

"No, not after the lawyer's 'just over a thousand' turned out to be nearly eighteen hundred, the cheeky sod," said Linda. "And after I'd buttered him up too."

I finally sipped my tea. "Anyway, it's early days yet. Let's see how we feel after spending the winter there. We might decide we prefer to be nearer the coast."

Bill scowled. "Not me. I've no desire to be down there living cheek to cheek with a bunch of heathens."

"And far from your dear Alberto."

"Paul wouldn't want to be near the coast," I said. "He hates busy roads."

"Me and you could go, Sue, and leave these two up in the hills. Pina coladas at sunset by the sea every evening, taking our pick of all the young gigolos."

"Yes, Linda, but I like the village." I sighed. "I expect Paul will be done with work altogether in a couple of years, then we can decide if we want to sell up. Do you think we'll miss anything about home?"

"The garden, maybe, but I can live without it," said Linda.

"Given that the libraries have practically stopped investing in serious books I can't think of a single thing that I'll miss," said Bill.

"What about our friends?" I said.

"They can come to see us and we can stay with them whenever we come back," said Linda. "It'll be better that way. Absence makes the heart grow fonder and all that."

"I'll miss seeing Lucy and Lewis," I said, referring to our grandchildren. "But I see far less of them than I'd like anyway. Maybe our kids will value us more when we're in Spain."

"Luke's already angling for an invitation," said Linda.

"Is he still in France?"

"I think so. He got sacked from the kayaking job when they found out how useless he was at it, so he went to stay with an old girlfriend near Bordeaux."

"Would that be Annie?" I asked.

"That's the one."

"Oh, are they back together?"

"Er, no. She's married to a Frenchman, so God knows what the poor chap thinks of his visitor."

"I think Luke's biding his time down there so he can go to Spain when we arrive," said Bill, shaking his head.

"I'll be glad to see him, for a while," I said.

"Yes, for a short while," said his mum.

A couple of weeks later Paul came home from work and declared that he planned to be done there within six months.

"Oh, why's that? I don't mind coming back here with you when you have to."

"Do you remember a chap called John who we spoke to at the last Christmas do?"

"Yes, and his wife, er... Sarah."

"Well Sarah's just become a widow, I'm afraid."

"Oh, God. What... was it?"

"Cancer, galloping cancer. Diagnosed a month ago and he died yesterday. We found out today. We had no idea he was so ill. Only fifty-five and he always looked after himself." He shook his head and sniffed. "Nope, time waits for no man, Sue, and I'm not working for longer than I have to. We'll be comfortably off and I'm going to finish as soon as I can. If it was any old job I'd quit today, but I can't leave them in the lurch. I've already told Des that I'll do another month full time then come back when they need me until next Easter, then that's it."

"Did he understand?"

"Perfectly. So, you can book the tickets for any time after the… fourth of October, and tell Bill and Linda to book theirs if they haven't already. Have they found tenants for the house yet?"

"Not yet, but the agency will find some. They charge through the nose but they have a good reputation. Maybe we could use them after Easter."

"Hmm, we could, or we could look into buying a place, don't you think?"

"Yes, but as Linda often says, let's go with the flow."

"OK." He moved his head from side to side until his neck cracked. "I'm going out on the bike for an hour, love. It's been a stressful day."

We soon booked our single tickets to Alicante and began to visit all the people we wouldn't be seeing for a while. Our daughter Emma was based at a youth hostel in the Peak District, so we spent a night there, before driving down to Luton to see our son Adam and his family. Emma approved of our move and Adam didn't seem to mind either way. Linda and Bill brought their more valuable items to our house and just before we left they met their tenants, a pleasant couple with a twelve-year-old and not overly destructive-looking son, Linda said. At the end of September they sold both their cars, so I also sold mine in an act of solidarity. Poco a poco we were severing our ties with the Old Country.

# 8

"Ah, a couple more weeks and I'll be in my seventies," Bill said as the plane flew over the Bay of Biscay.

"Salads for you every day then," said Linda.

"No need. I'll be stepping up the walking right away. Alberto says he's in training too, although all that work at the pool kept him pretty fit."

I chuckled and Linda tutted.

"I hope my bikes'll be all right," said Paul, as two of them had been added to Linda and Bill's consignment of items due to be delivered within a few days.

"One's in the super-duper case and the other's an old one," I said.

"Land ahoy!" Linda shrieked, scaring the old lady by her side. "Sorry," she murmured, before leaning over Bill.

"The Cantabrian Coast, I believe," said he. "Bathed in sunlight today, but it rains a lot up here in autumn."

"Well we'll be down south in two ticks. I can't wait."

As Bill is a great one for planning ahead and avoiding unnecessary costs, he'd arranged to see some cars at a Seat dealership just a short taxi ride from Alicante Airport, so two hours after arriving he was driving us up the motorway in their new three-year-old blue Seat Leon saloon car which we were all insured to drive. It was a warmish, sunny day and it wasn't until we passed the closed village pool that it dawned on me that summer really was over. Although Linda and Bill were the ones who were effectively emigrating, it felt like a decisive step for Paul and I too, as we intended to pay only the briefest of visits home until he retired. With our pool afternoons a thing of the past and no garden to tend, I wondered how I'd fill my time, but I needn't have worried because Linda was already on a mission.

I'll spare you most of the usual settling in details, save to say that after much debate Linda agreed to kick her 'soap' habit and we settled for a smart TV and a Netflix contract to get our fix of programmes in English, although we vowed to watch the Spanish channels most of the time. We furnished Bill's study on the second floor, bought some comfy Ikea chairs for the small parlour downstairs, and left Aunt Jean's studio untouched until we came up with a worthy idea for its use. As we still didn't know what to do with her ashes, Linda and I tracked down her husband Juan's son, also called Juan, who lived in a nearby village and continued to work the family land. The middle-aged farmer's taciturn ways and inability to maintain eye contact reminded us of his father forty years ago and he had no suggestions to make regarding Aunt Jean's remains.

"Do you think she would like us to scatter the ashes on your land?" I said, having prepared the question earlier, mainly because they looked so happy in the photo among the flowery almond trees.

He shrugged. "Do so if you wish, but don't get it near the trees. Human ashes contain a lot of salt. Very bad for the trees."

We bade him good day and decided against it.

"Miserable git," Linda said in the car.

"Maybe we should scatter them from one of the mountains she used to paint," I said.

"Er, yes, but how will we get there?"

I lifted a foot and patted it. "Bill can take us when he's explored the hills with Alberto. Anyway, we can't swim now, remember, so we'd better do some walking too."

"Yes, but our number one priority is to find a victim or victims for our exchange classes," she said with a cackle, this being the aforementioned mission.

"I'm not sure how well they'd work, Linda. Wouldn't it be better just to find a Spanish teacher?"

She tutted. "Don't forget that we're poor pensioners now, Sue. We can't afford to splash money around. We could put an advert in the shops and bars and see who applies."

"Applies?"

"Well, expresses interest. The idea is that we speak Spanish for half the class and English for the other half. It'll be a way to meet people too. The neighbours are polite but I bet they're ever so curious about us really. Whoever becomes our privileged, er… exchangee will have access to our innermost secrets."

"Yours, perhaps. We'll write the advert then and see if anyone bites."

"They'll be chomping at the bit, you'll see."

We composed and printed the advert and all four establishments were happy to pin it up, even the all-male bar where we dared to stay for a quick coffee, at a table of course.

Weather-wise we'd been lucky, because we'd missed two huge downpours at the end of September and the October weather was benignly sunny. Paul hit the road whenever it suited him and he looked forward to riding with the mysterious Arthur. As his phone remained switched off Paul dared to approach his 'little place' and the security guard told him that his boss would be arriving at the beginning of November, all being well.

"All being well?"

Paul frowned. "Hmm, yes, that's what he said. It was the same chap as before. Last time he looked very alert and military, but today I noticed he was unshaven and sort of slouched up to the gate. I guess it's because Arthur's not there, but he... well, he didn't seem very happy. You'd think he'd be chuffed to have the run of the place, but he looked sort of down in the dumps."

"Perhaps he had a hangover."

"Could be. Arthur told me he had a lot of good wine in his cellar in the basement, even though he doesn't drink it himself. Oh well, I'll call him in November."

Bill lost no time in contacting Alberto and the stout, florid chap often came to the house to whisk his pal away in his ancient Toyota 4x4. Bill usually returned looking pleasantly tired and smelling slightly of drink, but he explained that after a ten kilometre hike a man had to 'tomar algo' – take a little something – in order to rehydrate.

"If it weren't for your scuffed and dusty walking shoes I'd suspect you'd spent the whole morning in a bar," Linda said on his return one day.

"Au contraire, my dear. We walk up and down at least one big hill before eating a big *bocadillo* and washing it down with a beer or two. It may be the brandy from the restorative *carajillo* that you can smell on my breath, but it complements the coffee."

"So do you speak Spanish with him now?" I asked.

"Hmm, un poco, but he does like to rattle on in Yankee about his travelling days. He speaks it so well that it's hard to switch to Spanish, but we do occasionally."

I glanced at my sister. "Are you still planning to go on a trip with him?"

"Oh, yes, that is, if my better half allows me."

She regarded him sternly. "It's the booze I'm worried about, Bill. You can say what you like, but Alberto's a lush if ever I saw one. One thing's going for a spot of *almuerzo* after your walks, but if you're with him day and night I'm concerned that you'll overdo it and get into some kind of scrape."

He smiled and squeezed her shoulder. "Nonsense, dear. We're both mature, responsible, married men."

"Hmm, I'm not convinced. I can't stop you going, but it'll have to be just a few days and not too far away."

"Yes, well, we were thinking about the Sierra de Segura, only a couple of hundred kilometres inland from here."

She frowned. "We'll see, but I'll be monitoring your breath every time you come back from one of these hikes."

"Aye aye, Ma'am," he said with a little salute, before trotting nimbly up the stairs.

"I think they'll be all right, Linda."

"There'll be some kind of cock-up along the way, you'll see."

"I doubt it. Come on, let's go for a quick drink before lunch."

In our usual bar we'd got to know a young waitress called Nieves quite well. The cheerful, solidly built village girl spoke Spanish to us more slowly and clearly than anybody else and she was impressed by how much we'd improved.

"We understand you, Nieves, but not many other people," I said in Spanish.

"Don't you want to learn English, Nieves?" Linda asked, pointing to our advert.

She blushed. "Oh no, not me. I was bad at English at school. Just a few words for the tourists is enough. When I have tried to speak more to them they think I speak it well and start to speak fast, so I only say important words now."

"Is anybody interested in our classes?" I asked.

"I don't know, but many people have looked at the advert."

"In one week only one person calls. He was a silly man who… yes, a silly man," said Linda, unable or unwilling to explain that the jovial caller had said something about massages, perhaps believing the advert to be a veiled offer of some other kind of services, though she suspected he might have been having a joke, maybe in the other bar with his pals.

Nieves smiled. "I'm sure someone will wish to do the classes with you."

"We hope so," I said.

"We are keen to start," said Linda.

Just then the postman came in and spoke rapidly to Nieves for a while before handing her a letter and leaving. We caught hardly a word.

"Nieves, is he speaking Valenciano?" I asked, too rattled to remember my tenses.

"Him? No, Castellano," she said, meaning Spanish.

We shook our heads. With Nieves and a couple of other forbearing people we could now communicate, but we still had an awfully long way to go.

Linda sighed. "It's a pity the postman and other folk don't have pause and rewind buttons. Perhaps Paul was right and we're too old to learn it."

"I don't think we'll ever be fluent, but we can still improve a lot."

When Nieves passed by our table Linda asked her if she'd seen the English couple on their last visit.

"Not much. They came here only once, I think, with the old man who was with them in summer. They were very quiet and didn't stay long. I think they stayed in their house and had no parties."

"Did they have expensive cars?" I asked.

"Just a normal one, I believe. Yes, they were different this time. Perhaps a little sad."

"Do they say when they return?" Linda asked.

"Not to me." She went back to the bar.

"Perhaps they've fallen on hard times," I said.

Linda chuckled. "Maybe the bottom's fallen out of whatever market they deal in. They might even be in prison."

I shook my head. "Do you still believe they're criminals? They seemed all right to me."

"Oh, I don't know. A bit shady maybe, but nothing sinister. Shame really, as I was looking forward to a shoot-out at their corral."

"Well, we'll see them when they come."

"No word from Anke?" she asked, as our friend usually emailed me.

"She's still in Holland with her son and his family. She thinks she'll stay until Rik gets back from Nigeria."

Linda finished her small glass of beer. "Oh, I do hope we get someone to do classes with soon. We're in danger of becoming directionless."

I laughed. "Don't be daft. We're still finding our feet. Speaking of feet, we're going for a proper walk this afternoon."

"In the park?"

"Linda, the park's a hundred yards long."

"We have to get there and back too. It all adds up."

"To about a mile if we walk up and down a few times. No, we're going to walk up the road for, er… twenty minutes, then back down it. We'll do a bit more every day."

She groaned.

"It's a healthy pursuit, Linda."

"We might get knocked down. That wouldn't be very healthy."

"Knocked down by what? We'll probably only see about two cars and a tractor. Come on, time for lunch."

About a week later we were finally contacted by a bona fide exchange student. She spoke quite quickly in Spanish on the phone, but Linda managed to arrange a meeting in the bar for six in the afternoon.

"What about our walk?" I said, as we were up to an hour by then and feeling better for it.

"We're due a day off and it might rain anyway." She tapped her head with her fist. "It's time to use this now."

When a large lady with dark permed hair and a pleasant face entered the bar we'd already fortified ourselves with half a glass of white wine. I stood up and invited her to our table, but before sitting on the proffered chair she took a deep breath and delivered a little speech in extremely Spanish-sounding English.

"Hello, I am Ana. I live in Muro de Alcoy but I am from Murcia. I am fifty-two years old. I have two children, a husband and a cat. I work in a hotel in Alcoy and I need learn the English better for my job." She then exhaled noisily and laughed.

We chuckled, introduced ourselves in English, and after kissing we finally sat down.

"What would you like to drink?" I asked her.

"Black coffee for me, please. I am on the regime."

I ordered it and two more wines. Ana was friendly but quite loud and intense, so I thought we might need them.

"The bar will be quiet now for an hour," I said slowly. "Shall we have a little class today?"

She raised her hands, let them fall, and grinned. "Why not? But my English is very *very* bad."

"Don't worry, our Spanish is also bad. So, shall we speak English for half an hour, then Spanish after?"

She nodded vigorously. "OK, yes, good." She gazed at us expectantly. Even Linda seemed lost for words.

"Er, well, we haven't prepared anything, so we can just talk," I said.

"Yes, good, just talk, yes." She sipped her unsweetened coffee and smacked her lips. "To talk is good. Hablando se entiende la gente, eh?" she said, meaning that people understand each other by speaking. It has occurred to me that the best way to reproduce the linguistic mishmash which follows is to put the Spanish speech in italics, so here goes.

"So, Ana, why did you come to live in this area?" I asked.

She smiled and nodded. Though overweight she was an attractive lady who applied her make-up with care and obviously took pride in her appearance. She wore a billowing blue dress of expensive material and tasteful flat shoes on her rather large feet. Her broad face was expressive and now expressed intense thought. I was about to prompt her with a more specific question when she began to speak. Now, over a year later, I can still remember her initial discourse vividly, though not word for word, of course. It went something like this.

"My husband Miguel I meet in Murcia when he work there many years ago. He is, how you say, *a workman who lays bricks and does other similar tasks?*"

"A bricklayer," Linda said.

"Say again, please."

"A brick-layer." She mimed a nifty bit of trowel work.

"Yes, a brick-liar, so, I meet him there and we in love so a year later we married and come here to cold Muro de Alcoy." She shivered. "I Murcia girl and the winter there not so cold. Here, *here my feet still freeze in the street when it's really cold*, very cold."

I raised a forefinger and reproduced her Spanish sentence in English.

"Feet freeze street, yes, so I come here and have baby girl then boy then I think, oh, I need work now, so I go... *I go from place to place asking for work but that was a bad time*, a bad time, but later opens the hotel and they need people, so I get job ten years now and... *and to be honest it's the best job I've ever had as it's easy work for me in reception, but now they say I need to improve my English*, my English, so when friend here tell me you want the classes I... *call*."

"Call, or telephone," I said.

"Ah, yes, call, I forget."

Linda drank half a glass of wine.

"That's interesting, Ana. So, what you said in Spanish just now–"

"Yes, it good job and husband and me happy here, but oh *I miss Murcia and go to visit my family and friends when I can*, when can. The people here is a little... closed and in Murcia they more sympathy and–"

"Friendly," I interjected sharply. Me being a teacher, and an English teacher to boot, meant that this bilingual stream of consciousness stuff simply wasn't on. "The people are more friendly. Sympathetic is when you feel, er... compassion."

"Yes, Murcia people more friendly, *although* people all right here also. Now, last four five years more foreigners come to hotel so my boss say, Ana, come on, you English not too good, *you need to be able to hold a conversation and tell the guests about the local attractions*, so I say, yes, yes, I start the class and learn more soon."

I hope the italics have conveyed Ana's gung-ho approach and I won't inflict any more of it on you for now. This went on until half past six on the dot, as Linda had been glancing at the clock for a good ten minutes.

"...and my back *hurts a lot* because of my big *breasts*, so maybe I have *reduction* operation soon."

"OK, it is half past six, so now we can speak Spanish," Linda said in Spanish. "Nieves, the same again, please."

"Wait a moment," I said in English.

"No more wine for you?"

"Yes, more wine, but before we start to speak Spanish we have to talk about some of the things you said in Spanish, Ana."

She smiled and nodded. "Yes, yes, Sue."

"Next time I will bring a notebook and make notes, but now I remember you said… oh, I can't remember what you said."

She swatted the air. "Ach, it doesn't matter," she said in Spanish. "Now it's your turn to speak for half an hour. I'm not worried about little mistakes. I just want to practise my English."

"Yes, but..."

"Good, Spanish now," said Linda. She sipped her fresh wine. "I now live in this pretty village. I like this village a lot. We have a big house, two husbands and a car." She looked at me.

"My husband Paul likes cycling. He rides for many kilometres on his bicycle. He still works in England a little, but will retire in a few months," I said, correctly, as I'd been rehearsing ever since Ana's call that morning. "Linda's husband is called Bill."

Linda patted my hand and shook a finger at me. "My husband Bill likes to study a lot. He likes history and other interested things." Ana just nodded. "He goes walking with his friend Alberto. Alberto works at the swimming pool here in summer." She tapped my hand.

I had plenty more stock phrases, as did Linda, but I suggested Ana ask us a few questions.

"Bien, er, what was your work in England? She said slowly.

Linda gave me the nod.

"I was a teacher, an English teacher," I said pointedly. "I worked in a school in my town for about thirty years. I liked it, but now I like it here in Alicante." I glanced at my sister.

"I was an accountant, more or less. I worked in one company for a long time and other for a short time. I finish in June."

"I finished," I said, as Ana was still nodding happily away.

"Gracias. I finished in June."

"What did the companies make?" Ana surprised us by asking.

"Er, my first company make... *furniture*." (Now the italics are for English until further notice.) "They make... no, made, beds and tables and chairs and *wardrobes* and... more things. It was a good, *well-paid* job."

"Why did you leave?" Ana asked.

"Oh, the factory moved to another town, *because the rent was cheaper*. It was long distance to drive, so I find a new job in a *travel company* in my town. I worked *less than before* and it was good."

I chuckled. "We must bring notebooks to our next class."

Both Linda and Ana nodded vaguely and we carried on. I tried to avoid falling into the vice of inserting bits in English, but I soon found that it was a tremendous help in making the sentences flow. Ana corrected about three of the dozens of mistakes we must have made and I resolved to have a serious chat with Linda after the class.

Shortly after seven Ana said she had to go and she asked us if we'd like to meet at the same time the following week.

"Yes, but can we meet at five o'clock so we will have more time before it gets busy?" Linda said in English.

Ana grinned. "Claro, of course, the hour it go very fast." She beckoned the young waiter called Fran over, as he'd relieved Nieves during our 'class'.

"We will pay, Ana. You drive here," I said in Spanish.

She shook her head and tutted about a dozen times. "No, no, I paying today."

Thus began a bilingual tussle which we eventually won.

"We can come to Muro next week if you like," I said in Spanish.

"OK, yes, but to my flat," she said in English. "This bar I like, but in Muro better my flat."

"We can also do class in our house one day," Linda said in Spanish.

"Oh, I like that, yes, to see you house." She pushed herself up. "Oh, I am so fat. I do regime, but it is hard."

We walked her to her car and after farewell kisses we waved her off.

"Well, she's very nice, I must say," said Linda, before hiccupping.

"Yes, but we can't have more classes like that one."

"What was wrong with it?"

"Oh, come on, Linda. We chopped and changed like I don't know what. No, we'll have to stick to the language we're speaking and make notes and correct each other."

"Ach!" she said, just like Ana. "I liked it like that. I was making mental notes of my mistakes anyway."

I laughed. "For instance?"

"Wardrobe, rent, travel company, er... less than. I know furniture is muebles. I just forgot in the heat of the moment. Do you remember the words you didn't know?"

"Yes, I think I do. Oh, well, it wasn't a complete waste of time then."

"Course it wasn't. If you want to make notes, make them about our stuff. I don't think Ana's all that bothered about speaking properly. She just wants to speak to the tourists. I think it's a social thing for her too."

"Hmm, all right, but I'm going to make some effort to correct her."

"Please yourself." She hiccupped. "Damn it, Bill'll know I've been drinking."

Her husband did indeed perceive the aroma of white wine and determined to make hay while the sun shone, or tease Linda while she hiccupped.

He gazed at her dolefully and clasped his hands. "I don't know if you two were thinking of ever taking a trip, but I'd be very concerned if you did. Having a class and drinking a little is one thing, but to be away for days and nights together is another matter. Sue's obviously a lush and you're bound to get into some kind of scrape, ha ha."

"Ha ha," I echoed.

Linda just hiccupped.

# 9

The following Wednesday we drove to the compact little town of Muro de Alcoy, a couple of miles to the north of Cocentaina. The Seat's swish Spanish-speaking navigation system led us to the newish block containing Ana's airy, spacious apartment which she proudly showed us around, speaking her usual mixture of English and Spanish. The class proved to be similar to the first one, except that I interrupted Ana brusquely whenever she made the same mistake for the second or third time. When it was our turn to speak Spanish I made notes which we would later peruse, so by the end of the class I didn't feel nearly as frustrated as after the first one. The following week we hosted the class, but after that we settled on our bar as the best venue, because Ana liked it and our meetings had become social occasions as much as classes. We finally felt that we'd made a Spanish friend to rival Bill's Alberto. I'd left the adverts up in the hope that more serious students might present themselves – to complement our sessions with Ana – but after our third class I took them down, as despite our unorthodox method we were making progress.

In the meantime Paul cycled, read, did some DIY and sometimes came walking with us, while Bill studied, walked, socialised with Alberto and also did a few domestic tasks. On the second Monday in November Arthur called Paul and he spoke to him in the parlour.

"Well?" I asked him afterwards.

"He got here yesterday. He wants to go for a ride tomorrow. I suggested meeting him in Gorga but he wants to meet here."

"Oh, so will we finally meet him?"

"Er, no. We're meeting near the park." He looked pensive.

"Is anything wrong?"

"Eh? No… no, I thought he'd be delighted to be back, but he seemed a bit subdued. Maybe he was sleepy or something."

"You once said you thought he might be foreign. Did you find out about that?"

He chuckled. "Yes, he's from Lincolnshire. He more or less admitted that he'd worked on that posh accent of his and it sort of slips a bit sometimes, especially when he's out of breath. I guess in the circles he moves it suits him to seem posh. We normally talked about cycling and bike stuff though, so I still don't know much about him. Still, I'm glad he's here. Apart from riding with a couple of Spanish lads one day I've been solo since we got back."

"Invite him in for a drink. Tell him we won't be too inquisitive. I'll make sure of that. He must get lonely in his house, unless his security guards are friends too."

"No, I once asked him and he said their quarters were round the back of the house through a separate door. He doesn't like to mix business with pleasure, he said."

"He seems like an odd man, Paul."

"Each to their own. I wonder how fit he'll be?"

The next day Paul returned from their ride looking extremely fatigued. To his surprise Arthur had arrived in a modest hire car and after assembling his flashy bike they'd headed south-west to Jijona and come back up the Sella road via a place called Busot.

"Fifty-six miles and hard all the way," Paul said after towelling himself down. "The bugger's as fit as a fiddle and as brown as a berry. Do you know where he's been for the last month?"

"Er, not London."

"No, in Morocco, in the Atlas Mountains, riding the roads and trails with a guide." He puffed out his cheeks and exhaled. "These hills are nothing to him now."

"He is younger than you, remember."

"I remembered today. I invited him here for a drink, by the way, but he preferred to shoot off. We're out again on Thursday and he's coming here in the car again."

"Why's that?"

"Oh, he says he's bored of the same old roads and wants to head further south and west like today." He shrugged. "Seems a bit daft really, as he doesn't live that far away, but I don't mind."

"And was he still as subdued as when you spoke on the phone?"

"No, he seemed OK, but we didn't talk all that much."

Bill stomped into the sitting room. "The danger has been averted, for now," he declared.

"What danger?" I asked.

"Our Luke. It turns out that after the Frenchman got fed up of him he was heading this way like a guided missile, but he stopped off to see an old friend in Barcelona. This friend says he might find a few English classes on the side, so he may be staying there for a while."

I smiled. "But he gets ever closer."

He sighed. "Yes, this fortuitous friend has merely put off the inevitable, I'm afraid. Next stop here, he assured me in his email."

"What's his Spanish like now?" I asked, remembering that he'd studied it at university.

"I've no idea, but no doubt he'll be practising it."

"It might be a good thing to have him around then. We can pick his brains. Are you speaking much Spanish with Alberto?"

He smiled. "Un poco más, sí," he said, holding finger and thumb an inch apart.

"We still haven't heard you talking to anyone yet."

"Well, I'm not quite ready to unleash my Castellano on the general public."

"Chicken. You too, Paul."

He shrugged. "I can greet people and ask for things. What more do I need? I'm off for a shower."

On Wednesday morning the young man from the hotel called at the house. We'd seen him around and knew he was called Carlos, but we'd only greeted each other briefly since our stay there back in the spring. I was determined to speak Spanish to him now that we were neighbours, but his news was of such a mysterious nature that I soon forgot to insist on my linguistic rights.

"Can I come in for a moment, Sue?"

"Claro, Carlos. Adelante," I said, ushering him in.

"Hola, Carlos," said Linda.

"Hola, Linda. Er, I come because two big Englishmen are at the hotel, since last night."

"Ah," I said, not yet intrigued.

"These men they ask me a lot of questions," He frowned. "I don't like these men. Very big and bad, I think."

"What did they ask you?"

"They ask about Englishman here, or near here. I say there is none at the hotel, but they say, no, no, living here, or near here. I don't like them, so I say I don't know." His anxious expression cleared for a moment and he smiled. "I think fast and I say I don't live here, only work. They go to their room and I find Susana, the owner, and tell her about these men. She says OK, we tell them nothing. This is last night. This morning at breakfast they asking more questions and looking at me in bad way. Come on, they say, there *must* be English around here. They ask Susana also, so she pretend not to understand. Later she says to me, go to see the new English people and tell them."

Linda's eyes were open unnaturally wide. "They might have *followed* you here," she said in a hushed voice.

I sighed. "It's not funny, Linda."

"Sorry."

"No, they not follow me. I wait until they go away in car and then come here. Who do you think they look for?"

"Well..." Linda began.

"We don't know," I said sharply. "Carlos, if they ask you again just say you know no English people around here, OK?"

"OK." He scratched his nose. "Er, you not have problems with these men?"

"Of course not," Linda barked. "We're respectable people, entiendes?"

"Yes, Linda."

"How long are they booked in for?" I asked.

"Three nights, so two more. I glad when they go. Bad, rude men. I go back now."

I accompanied him to the door and peered up and down the street. "Thanks for telling us, Carlos. We will, er... think about who they might be looking for."

"OK, bye, Sue."

I found Linda in the study with the boys. Paul had been using the laptop while Bill read, but Linda's news had put a stop to that.

"… so it must be Wayne they're after," she said, flushed and excited. "Carlos said they said in or near the village, so that points to him, and Kerry too maybe. Oh, they'll ask and ask and then lay in wait for them when they come back." She drew breath. "We might see a shoot-out after all."

Paul yawned. "There are quite a lot of Brits in this area."

"Yes, but not in or *near* this village. It's them all right. I mean, who else would two big nasty men be after? It stands to reason."

I gave her a stern teacherly look. "Linda, it sounds to me like you *want* it to be them. I thought you liked them."

She shrugged. "I do. They were nice about Aunt Jean. We have to protect them. Someone here must have their number, or we might be able to track down the man who looks after their pool."

"Yes, we can do that," I said.

She gritted her teeth and grimaced. "Ooh, and I bet those horrid men come here! Yes, someone's bound to tell them where we are, not realising they're evildoers. They'll batter down the door, I bet. They don't sound like the type who'd knock."

"Linda, put a sock in it," said Bill, as her animated speech had contained more than a hint of mirth.

She pouted drolly. "I'm only trying to cover all the angles, Bill."

Paul sighed and handed his mobile to me. "Sue, please call the hotel and tell them to let us know when these men get back."

"OK. Er, why?"

"Because I'm going to see them. I'll soon find out who they're after and we'll be able to act accordingly."

"But they might kidnap you, Paul," said the resident clown.

"Me? But I don't owe a penny to anyone."

"Do you think that's what it's about, debts?" I asked.

"Sounds that way to me. Look, if it was police business it'd be the Spanish cops who'd make enquiries first. I bet they're debt collectors."

"Maybe they're gangsters from a rival racket to Wayne's, here to bump him off," said Linda, but less effusively. "I'm not sure you should go, Paul. It might be better to call the police."

"And tell them what? Look, I'll just say that I'm the only Englishman around and see what they have to say."

Bill cracked his knuckles. "I'll come with you. I've no debts either and I doubt it'll be about the library book I forgot to take back."

"No, I'll go with Paul," I said. "A feminine presence might be a good thing."

"I'll come," said Linda, but we were unanimous in rejecting her kind offer.

I called the hotel and spoke to Carlos.

We were a sombre group over lunch that day and when Carlos called back at about three Paul and I skipped coffee and walked down to the hotel. Carlos called their room, as we thought it more prudent to meet them in the lobby, and within a minute two great hulking men in their mid-twenties with short hair lumbered down the stairs. They didn't look all that evil to me and they greeted us pleasantly enough.

"I hear you're looking for an Englishman," Paul said calmly.

The taller of the two men glanced at Carlos, who was shuffling papers, and suggested stepping out onto the street.

We led them out into the sunshine and over to a nearby tree. The other man wandered off and lit a cigarette.

"Lived here long, have you?" the man asked in a cockney accent which would have thrilled Linda.

"We inherited a house last spring and we've been living in it for the last month," I said with a smile.

"Right. Just the two of you?"

"No, her sister and husband too," Paul said. "We're from Staffordshire."

"Hmm, well, we've come from London looking for an English bloke. We know he's got a house around here and we need to talk to him."

Paul nodded and held the man's gaze. "What for?"

"He owes a lot of money. He keeps giving us the slip and our bosses are getting tired of it, so they've sent us here."

"Who are your bosses?" I asked boldly.

He looked puzzled. "A debt collection agency, of course." He smiled to reveal a set of impeccable teeth. "Ha, we're not gangsters or anything."

Feeling slightly more at ease, I allowed Linda to inspire me. "So what are you going to do to whoever it is?"

He grinned. "Just have a little chat and try to persuade them to pay up. By the look of it he might have to sell his property here to settle this debt, so part of our remit is to find out where it is and what it's like. We think he just rents his place in England, you see. Whenever we hear he's back in town we go to look for him, then he's gone again. He's a right headache, but Gary and me are used it to. We come to Spain a lot, mainly to the coasts. You'd be surprised how many people think they're out of reach here, but we tell 'em they either cough up or it'll become a police job. Most of them understand that. The lingo's not much of a problem on the coast, but here we're a bit stumped. Nice round here though. We're enjoying it so far."

I sensed that he was trying to lull us into lowering our guard and Paul clearly felt the same.

"There must be dozens of Brits in the valley, but we're the only ones who live in this village. Here there are Dutch, French and a Belgian, but just us Brits. We haven't had time to meet any of the ones around here yet. You could try the other villages."

"Yeah, we will." He scratched his clean-shaven chin and thought for a while.

Paul stroked my arm. "Er, whereabouts are they from in England?"

"Sorry, I can't divulge that." He smiled. "I mean, I believe what you've told me, but it's been known for folk to tip people off. It happens all the time, but I reckon this bloke's gonna have to sell up and settle up." He stretched his pink, muscly arms and sighed. "Oh, well, I guess we'll go for a drive and check out some other villages. Thanks for coming to see us anyway. I guess we'd have ended up on your doorstep at some point and not everyone likes the look of us."

I chuckled. "Don't get sunburnt."

"No, I'll put cream on tomorrow." He cupped his hand to his mouth. "Gary, let's go! See you, then."

"Yes, good luck," I said.

"We'll find him. We usually do."

Paul grasped my hand and led me away at a sedate pace, before glancing back a couple of times.

"He didn't seem so bad," I said. "I don't suppose they'll duff anyone up."

"I wouldn't bet on it." A car door slammed and he glanced round again. "Ha, the red Golf."

"We'd better try to get in touch with Wayne and Kerry, I suppose. They'll probably find out they have a house here before they go, but we weren't to know that, being newcomers," I said, feeling a touch of delayed anxiety. "Or it could be someone completely different. Shall we have coffee in the bar?"

"A quick one, then I'm driving over to Arthur's."

"Oh... oh, Arthur! I didn't twig. Do you think it's him?"

He shrugged. "Cockney debt collectors. Him going to Morocco for a month. Driving over here to go out on his bike, thinking they'd be watching for him there. That could have backfired on him. Do you know what I think?"

"What?"

"That they know he's a cyclist."

"How?"

"I don't know how, but I know that other bloke was looking at my legs," he said, Paul being the last person in the village to continue to wear shorts during the day.

"A gay debt collector?"

He laughed. "As you know, a lot of cyclists shave their legs, even though I don't bother any more. Arthur shaves his. I might be wrong, of course, but everything points to Arthur. They might even know that I know him, but I'll drive over and keep my eyes open for their car. That's why I wanted to spot it."

"Can you not just call him?"

He stopped and scratched his head. "Yeah, I suppose I could." He chuckled. "Maybe I'm getting carried away."

"Maybe Arthur's a thief and ought to be brought to justice."

"Maybe, but not by them. Their size isn't a coincidence, Sue. I'm sure they use strong-arm tactics and Arthur is a mate, albeit a strange one."

"He's got his security guard."

"He might make matters worse if he fancies taking them on."

In this account I've often poked fun at Linda's histrionic nature and fondness for intrigue, but I am her sister and do share those traits to some extent.

"Er, if you call Arthur he might... I don't know, fob you off and then barricade himself in or something."

"He might. That's up to him."

"But he might need help or advice and I doubt he's got anyone else to turn to. Why don't we both drive over and appraise him of the situation?"

He chuckled. "You remind me of your sister."

"I remind myself of her, but I'm not about to make a joke of it."

"It could be unpleasant. They might turn up when we're there."

"Then all the better if I'm with you. I'm sure they won't beat me up. He seemed too sensible for that."

"So shall I call him first, or shall we just go?"

"Let's just go."

He laughed. "OK, Linda."

"I know, I know. Oh, she's going to love this."

"Not now she isn't." He looked at his watch. "I bet they're upstairs having a siesta. Let's go and get the car keys."

So, after slipping into the house and grabbing the keys, sunglasses and hats, we drove to Gorga and from there to Arthur's house, which was just as large, secluded and fortified as Paul had described it.

"I'll leave the car pointing in the right direction, just in case," Paul said as he manoeuvred.

I fanned my face with my floppy hat. "I never expected excitement like this in Spain, I must say."

"Me neither. It's definitely going to be a one-off." He opened the door. "This is when the security chap appears from nowhere."

After peering through the gate for a couple of minutes it became clear that the security guard wasn't in residence. I pointed out that there was no car in sight either.

"He leaves them round the back. The window blinds are down, but I bet he's in."

"He's taking a risk going cycling, if it is him they're after."

"Probably can't resist it. I'll try the buzzer."

I'd expected Arthur's response to be slow or non-existent, but the gate began to roll open immediately. The front door opened and a dark, wiry, handsome man came bounding down the steps and across the gravel wearing a tense smile.

"Drive in and around the back, Paul. I'll open the back door for you," he said in his posh accent. He nodded to me before loping back inside and closing the front door.

We drove behind the house and parked up beside Arthur's hire car. He met us at the back door.

"Well, this is a surprise visit, Paul." He held out his hand to me. "Hello, I'm Arthur."

"Sue."

"Can you guess why we've come?" Paul asked.

He tittered. "An impromptu social call? Come in, come in."

We stepped inside and he double locked the door, before leading us into a huge, tastefully furnished and rather untidy sitting room.

"Take a pew on the sofa. A drink?"

"Do you have a beer?" I asked.

"I have everything, though I only drink water myself. Beer too, Paul?"

"Please."

"What are you going to say?" I murmured when he'd gone into the kitchen.

"I'll play it by ear."

"So, to what do I owe this unexpected pleasure?" he said as he placed our bottles and glasses on the low table.

Paul told him about the two men and our conversation with them in some detail. Arthur smiled, nodded and sipped his water.

"Hmm, and what makes you think they might be looking for me?" he asked so calmly that Paul began to fidget.

"Er, well, I just had a feeling they might be, that's all, and wanted to warn you."

Arthur's laugh matched his voice. "Haw, haw, Paul, how funny! I assure you that my financial operations are a little more... exalted than the ones those chaps deal in."

Paul sighed, apparently with relief. "Oh, that's all right then." He sipped his beer. "Silly of me, I suppose."

"Not at all, and I'm grateful that you saw fit to warn me."

"That's OK. Oh, where's your security man today?"

Arthur's smile didn't falter, but his left eyebrow twitched ever so slightly. I looked forward to telling Linda about that giveaway sign when I got round to reconstructing our interview for her delectation.

"I gave him the day off." He chuckled. "If truth be told I'm striving to be a little less tight about security nowadays."

"Hmm," said Paul, glancing around the untidy room.

I smiled as I gazed at the dusty wooden table, keen to do my bit.

"Are you enjoying your new life here, Sue?"

"Yes, it's great, but we're going back next week for a few days."

Paul drank some more, so I did too.

"I have to go to work."

"Yes, you said the other day."

Paul slapped his thighs. "So, nine o'clock tomorrow then, down by the park?"

Arthur grimaced and tutted. "Ah, I forgot. I was going to call you later. I can't make it tomorrow."

"Oh, that's a pity. Would you rather I rode over here?"

"No, as I say, I can't make it. I'll call you soon and we'll arrange another day."

I thought what Paul said next was a real brainwave, but he later confessed that he'd said it merely to prolong our stay and give Arthur a final chance to open up.

"Can Sue have a quick look at your bike collection?"

He smiled and his left eyebrow twitched again. "Ha, yes, but unfortunately it has become somewhat depleted. I had some of the newer bikes sent back to England, so I can enjoy them there."

"Oh, it's the vintage ones I like best anyway," he said, standing up.

"Come along then."

The security door to the bike room was open and I saw the stands where the missing bikes had been. The remaining eight just looked like old racing bikes to me, but I cooed appreciatively and asked him about a light-blue one without brakes or gears.

"Ah, that's my 1936 Bianchi track bike, reputedly ridden by the great Alfredo Binda, but I haven't been able to verify that. It's a valuable machine all the same, and one of my favourites."

Paul patted the old leather saddle, raising the dust. "It's a fine machine. So are your newer bikes in London now?"

"Yes."

Paul walked around to peruse a strangely shaped one.

"That's a 1948 Paris Galibier," Arthur told me. "Their frame design experiments never took off, but I suppose it was worth a try."

"Shame I won't be seeing them again," Paul murmured.

"What do you mean?" he asked.

Paul gazed at him and smiled. "Because you won't call me to go for a ride and I wouldn't be surprised if I never saw you again."

He looked rattled. "No, no, I'll call you soon. I enjoy our rides."

"I know, but I'm not stupid, Arthur. You're in some sort of trouble and we've come to lend a helping hand." He shrugged. "If you don't want to tell us about it, that's all right, but I warn you that those boys are going to comb the area and someone's bound to tell them where you are. There aren't so many English around here."

He smiled less stiffly. "Anglais? Mais je ne suis pas anglais. Je suis français, or rather French-Moroccan. In the village they know me as Alain, the Frenchman, so I have nothing to fear from those thugs, not here anyway. Come, let us have another drink."

Back in the sitting room he opened a cabinet to reveal a choice selection of spirits. Paul and I preferred another small bottle of beer, but Arthur, or Alain, poured himself a malt whisky.

"I'll just get some ice for this," he said as he left the room.

"Definitely a foreigner, putting ice in a good malt," Paul murmured.

We then made ourselves comfortable, us on the sofa and Arthur in an easy chair opposite.

He sipped his whisky and sighed. "I couldn't decide whether or not to tell you about my predicament, but I'm glad that I have. One has to trust someone, after all. The truth is that I've dug myself into a rather deep financial hole. In desperation I took out short loans with rather dubious providers and this is why those men are pursuing me."

"How do they know you're here?" I asked.

He shrugged. "I think they must have broken into my Docklands apartment. There's nothing incriminating there, but my guess is that they've seen some photos of this area and set their finest minds to work, finding out where it is."

"Were there photos of the house?" Paul asked.

"Good heavens, no. I'm not so careless. Just a few snaps I took when I was cycling."

"With your bike on them?"

"Yes, I fear so. A fine Pinarello I've now sold along with the other new ones, apart from the Colnago I ride." He sighed. "I hope they haven't trashed the apartment, as I'll have to sell it to pay off these dratted debts."

"Will you have to sell this place too?" I asked.

He smiled. "No, not this place, or my little bolthole in Marrakesh. Ah, Paul, you'll have to come to ride in the Atlas Mountains one day. I have a suitable bike you could use. It's a shame the Algerian part of the range is too dangerous to visit now, but there's plenty to go at in Morocco."

"Thanks, Arthur, but I don't really hang out with fugitives, or criminals."

"Criminal, moi?" he said with a laugh. "I have debts and I will pay them off, that's all. Fortunately my London home will cover them easily, then I shall live quietly and ride my bike."

"Will you pay off the debts that those two are after you for?"

"Of course, they'll be the first, then the banks, who are less persistent."

"Shall I tell them that?"

"You, Paul?"

"Why not? I'll just say I've tracked you down and that you'll be paying them off soon. Then they can go home."

This audacious proposal caused me no little anxiety and Arthur perceived this.

"Excuse me a moment."

"Don't get involved," I hissed. "He might not pay them, or they might insist on seeing him."

Arthur returned and placed a thick wad of euro notes on the table. "There's twenty thousand here, all they gave me for my beautiful bikes in Valencia. I'll pay the rest as soon as I've sold the apartment."

"How much is the rest?" Paul asked.

"It's about sixty thousand pounds altogether, but rises daily. I owe the banks around half a million. I thought my investments might recover, you see, so I've been putting off the inevitable. It'll be a relief to throw in the towel and live a normal life." He pointed toward the bike room. "How many bikes can a man ride, after all?"

Paul smiled. "We'll get back then and hand it over. Then hopefully you'll be able to come out for a ride."

Arthur drained his glass. "Oh, I couldn't ask you to do that. I'll drive over now and see them."

"We'll come and give you moral support," I found myself saying.

His subsequent laugh sounded rather Gallic. "If you like, Sue. I suppose it is a rather thrilling turn of events in a way."

I pictured Linda when she heard the news. She'd be sure to ask lots of questions.

"How come you have such a posh English accent, Arthur?"

"Alain is my name, Sue. Oh, before Morocco became independent in 1956 my parents went to live in France. They both came from colonial families which had become quite wealthy. I'm French really, but I like to think of myself as French-Moroccan because of our past, although I didn't actually visit Morocco until I was in my twenties. Anyway, I was born in Saint-Denis, near Paris, but was sent to a prep school in Hampshire for three years, principally to learn English properly. When I settled in London in the late eighties I found the plummy accent to be quite useful in opening doors." He chuckled. "I guess I've been a bit of a rogue over the years, like most people in the financial world, but I'll put that behind me now."

"Will you have enough to live on?"

"Oh, with this house and my flat in Marrakesh and the money I'll have left I'll be all right, though I shan't be able to collect any more really rare bikes."

"Get a titanium one," Paul said. "The frames last for decades."

"Ha, yes, I might do that. Shall we go then?"

On our way out Paul asked him if the security guards had been laid off.

"Yes, the last one left when I came back. Now that I'm about to become a normal citizen I think I can cast aside these paranoias of mine." He shuffled to a halt on the gravel. "If things had gone to plan I might have been worth fifty million, you know."

Paul patted him on the back. "The main thing is to have good health and be able to ride your bike in peace."

"That's very true."

The subsequent interview with the heavies took place in their bedroom and wasn't all that exciting.

"It's best this way, pal," said the taller one as he counted the euros on one of the beds.

Alain looked relieved to be taking this first step towards clearing his debts, but he just nodded.

"I'll never get in debt," said the other chap, Gary, who hadn't opened his mouth until then. He sounded rather stupid and I suspected that he delivered the blows when required.

"What about the Merc you've just bought?" said his colleague.

"That's nothing. I mean real debt. It eats away at you. You can go as far away as you want, but it still eats away at you. We see it all the time."

Alain smiled patiently. "Please tell your bosses that I'll put the apartment on the market right away and will clear the balance soon."

"The sooner the better, mate," said Gary. "The interest rates are bloody criminal."

I felt a Linda-like urge to butt in. "Did you break into his apartment?"

The taller man smiled. "We have specialists." He looked at Alain. "You'll find the door locked and everything fairly tidy."

"Thanks."

"Was it the photos that led you here?" I said.

Paul shook his head and smiled.

"Yep. That's not our line, but one of the girls recognised that place called Guadalest. Then I think she got on that Google street view thing and deduced that he must be on this side of the mountains. She reckoned he was a cyclist too. It's just a fluke that we came to stay in this village."

"We could have another week here," Gary murmured. "They needn't know we've found our man yet."

"Afraid not, Gary. We've got to get this cash back to base." He pocketed the notes and handed Alain a receipt. "I think that's it then."

We all shook hands like business colleagues and said goodbye.

"Nine o'clock tomorrow then?" Paul said in the street.

Alain beamed. "Por qué no?"

"What?"

I sighed. "It means why not. Do you speak Spanish well, Alain?"

"Yes, fairly well. It's quite similar to French in some ways."

"Please teach him a bit then. He's hopeless."

He laughed. "OK, I'll try. I'll ride over tomorrow, Paul, and we could come back past Confrides again. The roads are more pleasant that way."

"Yes, but go easy on me. You nearly killed me the other day."

"All right, less racing and more talking. I had things on my mind on our last ride."

We invited him for a drink, but he preferred to get back to send a couple of emails.

"I'll drop in another day. I'd better get the ball rolling, I suppose. Cheerio, then."

"Bye, Arthur, er… Alain," said Paul.

"Bye, Alain."

We decided to have one more beer before going home.

"Two big men were here asking questions," Nieves said, in Spanish, of course.

"We see them now and everything is OK. Dos cañas, por favor," I said, and to Paul. "Do you think Alain's told us the truth?"

"The whole truth and nothing but the truth? I don't know. I don't think he's a criminal, but one thing he said bothers me."

"What's that?"

"He said he didn't leave anything incriminating in his apartment. What do you suppose that means exactly?"

"Hmm, yes, incriminating regarding the loan sharks or the police. I suppose we should give him the benefit of the doubt."

Paul nodded and sipped his beer. "Yes, but I might be giving him the third degree tomorrow. For one thing it'll slow him down a bit, and I meant what I said about not consorting with criminals."

"Or fugitives, yes. Be subtle though. He seems all right to me."

"Con artists usually do, if they're successful. Oh well, he's only a cycling mate after all."

"Yes. Linda will be wondering where we've got to."

"I'm surprised she's not here looking for us."

"What will you tell her?"

He patted my arm. "You tell her, and ham it up for all you're worth. She's given up her soaps for the greater good, so the least we can do is give her a little titillation."

I giggled. "This third beer is giving me an idea."

A while later I assisted Paul into the house. He was wearing a sling made from four white napkins we'd borrowed and had covered his nose and most of his eyes with his free hand, as well as walking with a limp. Linda appeared in the sitting room doorway and her mouth fell open.

"Oh, my G*od*, Paul! What have the bastards done to you?"

He shrugged. "You should see the state of them," he whined nasally.

I'd covered my mouth and begun to sniff.

"Come in, come in. Let's have a look at you."

Paul hobbled in and Bill lifted his eyes from his book. He gazed at Paul and began to nod slowly. "Bashed you up, did they? Hang on, I'll just finish this page."

Linda gasped. "You heartless *beast*!"

"Oh, come on, Linda. Look at the state of that sling."

When she turned Paul stood smiling and slingless. "Better than EastEnders, eh?"

"Oh, you b...bugger! You scared me half to death." She took a deep breath and within about six seconds had composed herself. "Right, tell me *all* about it."

We sat down on the sofa and I set the scene of our initial interview with great dramatic effect, but Bill's sceptical gaze made me desist and tell it like it was.

"...so he'll sell his apartment and pay off the rest of his debts. That's about it, really."

Linda wrinkled her nose to denote disappointment.

"A rum character, this Arthur, or Alain," said Bill.

"It was quite harrowing, you know," I said, nettled by their equanimity. "I mean, it might not have gone as smoothly as it did."

"That's quite enough excitement for the time being, anyway," said Paul. "Back to normal now."

Bill slapped his book shut and smiled. "Not quite, amigos."

"Why not?" I asked.

"Because Luke's arriving next Monday."

"I thought he was going to teach English or something," I said.

"It appears not."

"We'll be in England when he comes."

"Don't worry, I'm sure he'll still be here when you get back on Friday."

"Worse luck," said Paul, who wasn't a big fan of his wayward nephew, or nephew-in-law as he liked to refer to him, although they got along well enough on a superficial basis.

"*Don't* let him take over the house," I said.

"How would he do that?" Bill asked.

"I don't know, but he has an uncanny way of pervading all the space he inhabits. Assign him a room and make him stick to it."

"He isn't bringing anyone with him, is he?" Paul asked.

"Not as far as I know," said Linda. "Though come to think of it he didn't say he *wasn't* bringing anyone."

"Please be firm with him, Linda. Remember there are four of us living here already," I said.

She flapped her hand. "Don't worry so. Just enjoy your time there, and please check on our tenants. When you get back we'll know what his plans are."

"That's what I'm afraid of," Paul said.

# 10

Paul returned home from his ride with Alain less tired than the previous time and convinced that he wasn't a wanted man.

"We talked a lot, even on the uphills, and everything he said seemed to add up. He was making good money in the City and it was only when he tried to get rich quick that things went pear-shaped. He mentioned us going to Morocco again."

"And do you fancy that?"

"Well, I wouldn't mind. It'd be different. It won't be for a while as he's busy sorting out his affairs. He expects to get well over a million quid for his flat in London, even selling it fast."

I smiled. "We might get as much as 300,000 for our house, you know, unless we decide to rent it."

"Hmm, the rent would be handy, but I think if we do decide to settle here I'd rather flog it. It'd be a pain worrying about tenants all the time, and whenever some little thing goes wrong the agency would charge us an arm and a leg. Still, it's early days."

"Yes, and we still haven't experienced a winter here."

He chuckled. "There's no sign of one yet, though I guess we ought to buy some firewood for the stove," he said, as we'd made do with the gas heaters to take off the chill up to then.

"Ana says it does get cold here though, compared to Murcia. We're quite high up and she says January and February can be 'freezy cold', I quote."

Paul smiled. "Well, she's not used to it like we are."

On Sunday the two of us flew back and caught a horrendously expensive taxi home from East Midland Airport.

"This is daft," Paul grumbled. "I think I'll sell the car and we'll hire one next time. It'll only be for a few days and the car's losing value all the time."

"Go ahead, but try to sell it on the last day. I want to drive down to Luton to see our long-lost grandchildren."

"OK, I'll look into it."

A friendly neighbour had been looking after our detached house and when we arrived the central heating was set at twenty degrees, which made me wonder if we really were used to cold weather, as the chilly bedrooms and hot-water bottles of our youth were but distant memories. In a way it felt good to be back and while Paul worked, I cleaned the house, tidied the garden and paid visits to a few friends. Our daughter Emma was busy in the Lake District, so I missed out on seeing her, but after a dreary drive down the busy motorway in the rain, my son and his family were pleased to see me and expressed polite curiosity about our new life in Spain.

"The house has plenty of space and you're welcome to come whenever you want," I told Adam and his wife Emily. "And there's a really great swimming pool near the village," I told Lucy and Lewis.

"Does it have a wave machine?" eight-year-old Lewis asked.

"Er, no."

He shrugged and resumed his perusal of his mum's iPad.

"So, is sharing a house with Aunt Linda and Uncle Bill working out then?" Adam asked, looking drained despite leaving work early.

"Yes, it's fine for now." I chuckled. "You cousin Luke will be there when we get back."

"Oh, God."

I said earlier that Bill was the antithesis of Paul, and the same could be said of Adam and Luke, only more so. Luke considered my son to be a company man and a slave to work, while Adam thought his cousin a shiftless, directionless wastrel with a grim future ahead of him. I didn't entirely agree with this, as although Luke's pension prospects would certainly be poor, my son's life appeared to be so stressful that I sometimes wondered if he'd reach retirement age with his mental and physical faculties intact. It was a pleasant visit though, and I promised to return in January with Paul.

The following morning Adam walked me out to the car. "We'll come out next summer, Mum, but I hope Luke's gone by then."

I laughed heartily. "Oh, he'll not be staying for anywhere near so long, I assure you."

He clamped his lips shut and nodded. "Hmm, I wouldn't be so sure about that."

"Don't be silly. He… he never stays in one place for so long."

"Because no-one'll let him. Bye then." We hugged and kissed. "Drive carefully."

On the motorway north I reflected on Adam's words and to put my mind at rest I made a hands-free call to Linda.

"Yes, he arrived on Tuesday, so only a day late."

"Is he well?"

"Yes, hairy, but well."

"Hairy?"

"You'll see. He's already made himself at home in the spare room."

"Has he brought a lot of stuff?"

"Just the usual massive rucksack."

"What's he been doing with himself?"

"Exploring the village and hiking to the other villages. He says he wants to get a feel for the place."

I gulped. "Has he, er… mentioned how long he might be staying?"

She giggled. "He has no onward destination in mind, if that's what you were hoping, but don't worry. I've told him to use the downstairs bathroom and pointed out that the house has its full quota of permanent residents."

"And what did he say to that?"

"He sneered. He said he wouldn't *dream* of living with his ageing parents. We'd cramp his style. He says that if he sees the area has potential he'll soon sort something out."

"Sort what out?"

"He was vague about that."

"Has he got much money?"

"Yes, surprisingly he's quite flush. He showed me his wad of euros to prove it."

"And is he… oh, I'll see him soon anyway."

"Did you call round at our house?"

"Yes, they're fine."

"Never mind them, what about the house?"

"Never been cleaner."

She snorted.

"They did say they may be moving out next summer though. He's after a job in Derby, so they might move over that way."

"Dammit. What a pain."

"We'll probably sell ours eventually."

"Yes, that might be the way to go. Oh, Bill's just got back. I'd better go and smell his breath. They're planning to shoot off somewhere soon, so I'm nagging him especially hard at the moment."

"Luke might want to go with them," I said hopefully.

"He might. Bye, Sue."

"Bye. Oh, how's Luke's Spanish?"

"You will soon see," she said in Spanish.

"Muy bien."

Not only did Paul arrange to sell his car, but he also suggested we look into selling the house.

"Already?"

"They sometimes take a long time to sell and we're not in a hurry like Alain. We could ask a good price and accept no offers, for now."

I thought about our carefully chosen furniture and all our other stuff. "Maybe next time we come, Paul."

"OK, it was just a thought."

I told him what I knew about Luke.

"Hmm, I'm glad he's got plenty of cash. Maybe he will find something to do there, and a place to live."

"Yes, it would be nice for Linda and Bill to have him close by."

"Yes, but not too close."

My friend and former colleague Dorothy drove us through the rain to the airport on Friday.

"You're welcome to come out whenever you want," I told her. "But I'd wait for the pool to open in June if I were you."

"I'll tell Frank and see what he says." She chuckled. "If you're not careful you might find you have a full house all summer long. It sounds lovely there."

As well as her and Adam and Emma I'd invited two more good friends and their husbands to visit. Paul hadn't invited anyone as yet, but he'd told some clubmates what a wonderful area for cycling it was. Linda and Bill had also invited a few people, so I feared that Dorothy might be right.

"We'd better furnish the spare rooms before next summer," I told Paul on the plane.

He smiled. "It's a long time till then."

As he enjoyed being enigmatic from time to time I left it at that. We saw very little all the way down through France, but the Pyrenees were a sight to behold. There the peaks pushed through the fluffy clouds and beyond them there was only blue sky.

"It's as if the mountains have held back the clouds," I said.

"I expect they have in a way, though I'm not sure what meteorological phenomenon it is. We should get good views all the way now."

We reached the coast somewhere to the north of Valencia and when the unmistakable tower blocks of Benidorm came into view we knew that beyond the mountains lay our new home. Paul said that he felt the 'noose of work slackening' and would be happy to leave them to it after Easter.

"Will you want to sell your share in the company at some point?"

"No way, I've worked hard there and I want to reap the rewards. I guess it's great for the Spanish economy to have all us Brits retiring here and spending all our hard-earned cash."

"Yes, but what about this Brexit business?"

"Bugger Brexit," he said, a year and a half having passed since the referendum. "People go to live in countries all over the world. They always have done. Anyway, the Spanish government wouldn't be stupid enough to scare us away. There are lots of

Spaniards in Britain now too. They'll come to some arrangement, you'll see."

"I bet it drags on," I said, and how right I was.

Linda and Bill were there to greet us at the airport.

"Where's Luke?" was the first thing I said.

Linda laughed. "Welcome back. He was too busy to come."

"Doing what?"

She smiled and sighed. "You'll see soon enough."

# 11

Luke was looking slim and healthy and the hairiness his mother had mentioned was concentrated mainly on his face, as although his brown hair was cut short, he'd cultivated a long and well-groomed beard.

"What's with the vegetation, Luke?" Paul said as he shook his hand.

His cheeky brown eyes gleamed and he raised his chin. "Don't you think it makes me look more dignified, Paul?" he said, as he'd long since dispensed with formal family nomenclature.

Paul gazed pointedly at his flowery shirt, ragged walking trousers and scuffed sandals. "It might, yes. What are your plans then?" he said, somewhat sooner than etiquette demanded.

Luke emitted his rather cavernous laugh. He's a tall, good-looking man and despite or maybe because of his footloose ways he's always enjoyed a lot of success with the ladies. The beard made his fine teeth look even whiter and I could guess the effect he'd have on the callow village damsels, if there were any.

"Right now I'm checking things out, feeling my way, talking to folk."

"How's your Spanish?" I asked.

"Getting better every day. I need to practise but I think I'll be up to speed soon," he said in clear and fluent Spanish.

"Muy bien," I said, to show I'd understood.

His mother grinned. "He's been teaching me some swear words and other slang."

"We won't need them," I said prissily.

"No, but it's good to know what people are saying. We're guiris, by the way."

"That's foreigner, isn't it?"

"Yes, but it's a bit derogatory. It's all right if they say it in a nice way, as a bit of fun, but I'll be listening out for it from now on and if anyone calls me guiri in a nasty way I'll call them an hijo de puta," she said, meaning son of a whore.

Luke raised his hands to his head. "Mum, please, swearing is still swearing in Spanish, you know."

"Mierda," she said, and burst out laughing. "That means shit, Sue."

"I know."

"I hope you're not approaching your second infancy, Mum."

"Not yet. Come on, you promised to buy us all dinner tonight."

In the bar Luke told us he'd been frequenting the other, scruffy bar in order to get to know the lay of the land.

"The blokes were a bit wary at first, because I don't drink alcohol."

"Or it might be the beard," said Paul.

"They might think you're a Muslim," said his dad. "Despite the fact that the Moors civilised much of Spain I believe they're not overly popular here these days. The other day I was reading an interesting–"

"But they soon warmed to me," Luke went on, more familiar than most with his father's rambling discourses.

"What do they say about us there?" I asked.

He shrugged. "Not much." He looked at Paul and Bill. "I think they wonder why you two don't go in for a drink."

"Alberto and I usually have a bite in other villages after our hikes."

"And a drink or three," said Linda. "And this one says he's not bothered about learning Spanish."

"Shame on you, Paul," said his nephew.

Paul shrugged. "These two are always at it and your dad's got his Spanish chum. I'm bringing up the rear, but my mate Alain's going to teach me a bit."

Luke knew all about Alain by then and despite the Frenchman's recent failure and his own loathing for bankers he admired his audacity.

"I'd like to meet this Alain, Paul. He might want to invest some of the money he's got left in some kind of business."

Paul frowned. "No, he won't. He's going to live within his means and ride his bike."

Luke shrugged. "I'm looking for a partner, you see."

"In what endeavour?" I asked.

"Not sure yet." He beamed at us all. "I just feel that despite the poor economic situation this is a land of opportunity." He inhaled through his nose. "I can feel it in the air."

"Since when were you a businessman, Luke?" Paul asked wryly.

He sighed and stroked the luxuriant growth that I had to admit was growing on me too. "I'm thirty-four next month, Paul."

"I know. And?"

"I always said I'd settle down when I reached thirty-four."

"When did you say that?" Linda asked.

He sipped his water. "Well, to be honest, it was this summer during the kayaking debacle. Luke, I said just after I nearly killed myself going down some rapids, it's time you settled down and put your nose to some grindstone or other. I was sacked the next day, so that clinched it. I didn't fancy Barcelona because this Catalan independence business means that they're always going on about politics, so it feels like fate that you've inherited a big house in this lovely village." Eyebrows were raised. "*But*, never fear, because I don't intend to stay with you for longer than I need to."

"That's a rather open-ended statement, Luke," said Paul drily.

"Don't worry, I won't get under your feet. I'm going to be tremendously busy until I find what it is I'm looking for."

Linda hummed that old U2 song.

"But you must have some idea of what sort of thing you want to do," said Bill.

He smiled. "Something outdoors, I hope."

"Involving tourists?" I asked.

"Maybe, maybe not. In some ways I'd like to ignore the tourist scene, but they're the ones with the money and I'm not so presumptuous as to think that I can beat the locals at their own game, or games."

"That's good to hear," said Paul.

"So, well, I've been out and about, chatting to folk and hoping to gain inspiration. These tapas are good, aren't they?"

"The best in town," Linda said.

Presently Luke called Nieves over to take our coffee order and his gallant manner made the poor girl blush. Something occurred to me.

"Er, Luke, I don't suppose you're hoping to shack up with some unsuspecting girl, are you?" I asked, as in the past the pursuit of a partner with her own residence had taken precedence over his projected occupation.

He gave me a saintly look. "No, Sue, that's not my intention. Once I establish myself in... once I establish myself, then and only then will I look around for a helpmate."

"Helpmeet," said Bill with teaspoon aloft. "Helpmate is a corruption of the word helpmeet." He frowned and lowered the spoon. "Or was it the other way around?"

"Whatever, Dad, but I mean it. From now on I shan't be diverted from my objective by, er... skirts, and I'd be grateful if you'd all put your thinking caps on and help me to come up with some good ideas."

"How much money have you got?" Paul asked him.

He beamed. "Altogether I've got about four thousand. I've never had so much money in my life and I don't mean to waste it."

Bill's brows rose. "How did you come by it?"

"I saved it, Dad. Since I stopped drinking last year it's just piled up."

"It's a handy sum, but not a lot of money to start something up," said Paul.

"I know. That's why I need a partner."

"Partners don't appear to strangers just like that," he said, now in Dragon's Den mode. "Do you know anyone anywhere who might back you?"

"Well, Terry, my builder friend in Ilkeston might be interested. It was when I was labouring for him that I saved most of my cash. He'd want to come out and see what's what though."

Sensing that the thin end of a wedge was about to be tapped in, I asked him what his friend was like.

"Steve's about my age and he's just split up with the missus. He's a good builder and he's doing well now that he's cut down on the drink." He smiled. "I helped him with that, by dragging him out of the pub before he got carried away. He might take a break and come over, he says."

Bill cleared his throat, but Paul was quicker off the mark. "Luke, we don't want anyone else staying at the house. With four of us it's just right and you're welcome to stay for a while, but another body would be too much. It's our home, you see, not just a holiday home, and–"

"Point taken, Paul." He smiled. "I'll get my own place before I invite him or anyone else to stay."

"Good, but if you rent somewhere now you'll soon run out of money. I... can I speak frankly, Luke?"

He unleashed is most disarming smile. "Of course, Paul."

"Well, I'm not convinced you'll find anything to do around here. If there were easy ways to make money, someone would have thought of them already. You speak Spanish, which is good, but you've no know-how here and you know no-one." He shrugged. "Go ahead and meet people and see what comes up. You never know, someone might offer you a job. Then you'd be able to save more and keep looking for opportunities."

Luke chuckled. "Wise words, Paul. Yes, I suppose I would take a job for now, but from what folk have told me there aren't any around here at the moment. Quite a few local youngsters have gone abroad to work." He sighed. "No, I reckon some lateral thinking is called for in this situation." He raised his hand. "Nieves, sweetheart, the bill, please," he crooned in Spanish.

The blushing girl brought it, tittered, and returned to the bar.

"Leave our Nieves alone, Luke," said Linda. "She's not for you."

"Don't worry, Mum. As I said, I shan't be deflected from my goal by the fair sex. I'm now a teetotal celibate and mean to make my mark on the world at last."

"Do you think Luke's really changed?" I asked Paul later in bed.

"I doubt it, not really, though cutting out the booze seems to have had a good effect. I never thought he'd manage to save four grand in his life. People like him don't make successful businessmen though. He'll need to find a job if he's going to stick around." He yawned, then smiled. "Down on the coast he might have better luck."

"I don't think he'll be any bother, do you?"

"Not on his own, no. He's a nice lad, but he's let himself down so many times that it'll take more than words to convince me that he'll ever amount to anything. Time will tell."

"Yes, I expect it will."

That Thursday morning Alberto came to pick up Bill in his dilapidated jeep and Linda insisted on him stepping inside, something he'd rarely done before. Paul was out cycling with Alain, but I was present to witness her pep talk.

"Please take a seat, Alberto. Coffee? No? All right, so, please tell me about your plans," she said, eschewing any attempt to speak Spanish in favour of clarity.

"I've already told you," Bill protested.

"I want to hear it from the hor… from Alberto's mouth."

Alberto sat with his back straight and his belly, which their hikes had done little to reduce, held taut. "Well, Linda, we're gonna drive to a lil place called Riópar where there's plenty of cheap rooms this time of year and do some walking. Then we'll drive down through the hills to a lil place called Segura de la Sierra. I reckon we'll camp out near there and do some more walking. Then, if the weather holds, maybe we'll drive down to a bigger place called Cazorla and walk some more. That's about the long and short of it, just a plain old walking trip." His subsequent smile looked uncannily American.

"I told you," Bill mumbled. He looked at me. "She's checking that our stories match."

Linda paced around with her arms folded. "Right, good, a walking trip, fine. So, do you intend to walk all day long, every day?"

"Well, Linda, once we start camping you'd be surprised how much time you spend setting up and cooking an' just moseying around. It's gonna be a fine break from civilisation for a few days. We'll come back looking mighty healthy."

"I weighed about eighty-one this morning and I'm gonna crack the eighty barrier before we come back," said Bill.

Linda frowned. "Gonna?"

"Yep." He shrugged. "We're *going to* be fine, Linda. We'll be back in a week at the latest."

"I wish Luke was going with you to keep an eye on you. Heck, I never thought I'd hear myself saying that."

"I invited him, but he says it's no time for a holiday now. Vamos, Alberto, let's hit the road."

"Is that old heap of yours reliable?" she asked the owner.

"Yes, ma'am, she a bit rusted but she runs like a dream. See y'all later then."

Bill hoisted on his new rucksack, kissed Linda and left.

"They'll be fine, Linda."

She sat down and shook her head slowly. "I don't know, I've got a feeling something's going to go wrong."

"I suppose they might break down, but car insurance here covers breakdown assistance, so they'll just get towed back." I chuckled. "We might see them sooner than we think. Luke's keeping busy, isn't he?"

She smiled. "Yes, he's caught the bus to Alcoy this morning. He's going to get his NIE number at the police station, buy a phone and then have a look around. He's no trouble, is he?"

"No, even Paul's impressed by the new, improved Luke. He doesn't seem to have any ideas yet though."

"No, apart from that daft one about parapenting or something. He'd kill himself as well as his customers."

"Yes, he'd be better off keeping his feet on the ground."

She stood up. "Come on, let's get to the market before all the good fruit and veg has gone."

"Vale," I said, meaning OK.

# 12

On Friday afternoon Linda and I went for our usual exercise walk. By now we'd dispensed with our out-and-back road route and instead followed one of three roughly circular circuits devised by Bill which used lanes, tracks and the odd scamper across almond and olive groves. On our way back along 'The Medium Walk' of about three miles we passed by Wayne and Kerry's chalet and saw a shiny red Ford Focus on the gravel driveway.

"They're here," Linda murmured as she peered over the gate.

"Yes. Why are you whispering?"

"Oh, I've still got my suspicions about them. They were red herrings in the Alain case, but that doesn't mean they're not dodgy."

I sighed. "Are you serious?"

"Not really. Well, only a teeny bit."

"Let's ring the buzzer."

"Are you sure?"

"Of course I'm sure. It'd be rude not to. I mean, they might have seen us."

She giggled. "I can tell you're dying to see them."

"They were nice about Aunt Jean and they're our only English neighbours," I said glumly.

She grinned. "You're classist, you are. Too hoity-toity to knock about with the likes of them."

I pressed the buzzer firmly.

Wayne soon loped over to the gate, his goatee wafting in the breeze and his head freshly shaved to reveal a blue tattoo I hadn't seen before.

He smiled. "Hello, girls, nice to see you." He slid the massive gate open with two huge fingers. "Come on in. Kerry's doing a spot of weeding. How've you been keeping?"

"Very well, thanks," I said.

"Great," said Linda. "Have you just arrived?"

"Last night. Just the two of us this time. Coffee? Beer? Something stronger?"

"We'll both have beer," said Linda.

"You'll find her just round there." He trudged into the house.

"I don't know if those two heavies could have coped with him," I said. "He's a giant."

"I bet he's a big softy really."

Kerry was kneeling over a flowerbed with her red tracksuit bottoms revealing the cleft of her considerable buttocks. I was pleased to see that she'd dyed her blonde hair back to brown again. She pushed herself to her feet and greeted us with a smile and a nod, before asking us how we were settling in.

"Just fine," said Linda. "How are you?"

She smiled weakly. "All right. Wayne's uncle has died. He was the old man you saw last summer."

We expressed our regret.

"Yeah, he'd been ill for a while. He came out with us for one last trip in September. He passed away about a fortnight ago. Heart disease, you know. So we've come alone this time, for a quiet stay."

In the expensively furnished living room Wayne told us that his Uncle Mike had taught him all there was to know about the markets.

"My granddad inherited a fruit and veg stall on the Great Homer Street Market and 'cause my dad went off to sea my Uncle Mike took it over and soon started expanding. I used to go and help out when I was a nipper and 'cause he didn't have no kids we've ended up running the show. We've got stalls right across the city now and twenty-odd people working for us."

"Still fruit and veg?" Linda asked after sipping her beer from the can, while I'd availed myself of the glass provided.

He chuckled. "Fruit and veg and clothes and bags and electronics. You name it, we sell it."

"Kerry grinned. "We've got our fingers in just about every pie now."

"Do you have children?" the inquisitive one asked.

"Just our lad Harry. He's at university in Nottingham."

"He's studying economics," said Wayne. "So that might be handy if he wants to come into the business."

"But I doubt he will," said Kerry. "He's never shown much interest really. Kids these days don't like getting up at four o'clock much."

We agreed that the younger generation lacked backbone and spent too much time prodding devices. I told them briefly about Adam and Emma, while Linda went into what I thought was unnecessary detail regarding Luke's ups and downs.

Wayne grinned and pulled his goatee. "Sound like a bit of a rascal, eh?"

"He was, but he's become more sensible now, we think," said Linda.

"And he's here," said I.

"How about if we meet up for dinner in the bar one night?" Kerry said. "We'd invite you here but we're sort of in mourning for Mike and don't really want to entertain here this time."

Linda smiled. "Oh, come to our house then. How about tomorrow night?"

They accepted graciously and we soon took our leave.

"We could have gone to the bar," I said when we'd got into our stride.

"Have you no sense of propriety, Sue?" she said with mock pomposity. "They'd have invited us to theirs had circumstances been favourable, so we must invite them to ours. You can tell you didn't go to finishing school."

"I just thought it would have been easier," I said lamely, as Linda had correctly perceived that I still felt a bit snobbish about associating with such gritty people, although I must say they never swore in our presence and Kerry's hair was a great improvement. Not socialising with people like them back home, however, was no excuse for not doing so in Spain, and as we genuinely liked them I told myself to embrace the opportunity of meeting folk from other walks of life. Besides, there's nothing duller than sitting around a table with several middle-class couples, more often than not talking about houses, other possessions and expensive holidays. In short, I vowed to dismount from my high horse and take a leaf out of Linda's book, although I wouldn't be drinking straight from a can for reasons of hygiene.

"Cool," said Luke when we told him about the dinner. "Market stalls, eh? Well I'll certainly be picking their brains then. Any word from Dad, Mum?"

She frowned. "Not even a text."

"There might not be a signal up there in the back of beyond. Shame I missed Alberto the other day. I'd like to pick his brains too." He chuckled. "You know, I'd never have expected you lot to meet such diverse folk. I thought you'd gravitate towards other boring oldies."

"We like meeting all sorts of people," I said, as the subject was still uppermost in my mind. "And from different countries. I think our Dutch friends will be back soon."

"Oh, yeah, the dredger bloke who's been all over the place. I'll definitely pick *his* brains."

"By the time you've finished, everyone's head will be mashed up," I said, pleased by my wittiness.

He grinned. "Maybe so, but I'll have some *ideas*, Sue."

"Nothing yet?" his mum asked.

He tutted. "Not really, and I've been told how damn hard it is to set up a business here. If you're self-employed you have to make a big payment every month, whether you earn anything or not. Then there's always all sorts of licences and other stuff. They certainly don't make it easy for would-be entrepreneurs like me."

"Something will come up, you'll see," said Linda.

"Is that one of your prophecies, like Bill and his friend getting into a scrape?" I said.

"Ooh, don't mention them, Sue. They're probably stuck down a ravine or something as we speak."

"They'll be fine, Mum. They just need to do some lads' stuff for a while."

Her eyes blazed. "What, like drinking and f…fornicating?"

He laughed. "I can't imagine dad fornicating, except with… no, I can't imagine it at all. Well, I'm off to the men's bar to chew the fat."

"And pick brains?" I asked.

"Oh, yes."

The Spanish don't usually eat paellas and other heavy rice dishes for dinner, Luke informed us, but we didn't think Wayne and Kerry would mind and we wanted to make something filling as they both looked like big eaters. Paul was pleased that we'd invited them and had even asked Alain along, but he'd declined, still being rather reclusive.

"He reads a lot, proper literature like you," he told me in our room. "But he needs to get out more and meet folk."

"Old habits die hard, I suppose. He'll be so used to being locked inside his house that he'll find it difficult to change. Maybe when he's settled his debts he'll loosen up a bit."

"Yes, hopefully. He mentioned us going to Morocco again this morning."

"Hmm, let's wait till Bill gets back first, shall we? Linda has a premonition that it won't go smoothly."

"That wreck of a jeep might break down, but apart from that what could possibly go wrong?"

"He hasn't called."

"Breathing space, Sue, breathing space."

"You know, I think Linda and I will plan a trip too," I said on the spur of the moment.

"Go ahead. We'll manage all right, I'm sure."

"Very well, I shall put it to her pronto."

Kerry and Wayne arrived right on time and were dressed so sombrely that there was scarcely a tattoo in sight.

"We find that we're thinking about Uncle Mike all the time," Wayne said after pouring his beer into a glass. "He came here with us a lot and this is where we spent most time with him. At work we'd be here and there and didn't see him that much."

"We were thinking about bringing his ashes here, but in the end we scattered them from the ferry along the Mersey," said Kerry.

"Not across the Mersey, like in the song?" Luke said.

"No, we went on a little cruise they do and found a quiet spot. We thought he'd have liked that more, though we had some great times here." She sighed. "I don't expect we'll have big parties like we used to any more. He was the life and soul of them. I'll be fifty next year anyway. Time to calm down a bit, I think."

"You look younger," Linda said truthfully, as her chubby face had few wrinkles.

"Aunt Jean's ashes are still here," I said, pointing to the mantelpiece. "We haven't decided where to scatter them yet."

"I know a place where she painted a lot," said Wayne. "A little ridge with a good view of the village. I could take you there if you like. It's not far from the road."

We accepted his kind offer before bringing in the big chicken and rabbit paella which we'd made on an especially wide gas burner Linda had bought. On tucking in our efforts were praised.

"Just as good as any we've had in restaurants," Wayne said as he shovelled it smoothly in.

"Delicious," said Kerry, a daintier eater.

"Very tasty," said Paul.

"I'm impressed," said Luke. "We could go into the catering business."

"We're retired and you can't cook to save your life," said Linda.

He patted his mouth. "No, but I'd get the contracts." He addressed our guests. "I want to set up a business here, you see, and I'm looking for ideas."

Wayne chuckled. "We looked into the markets here a few years ago, but they're tough nuts to crack, the proper markets, I mean. The paperwork's horrendous and you really need to be here all year round, so we knocked that idea on the head."

Kerry smiled. "I wasn't too keen anyway. We come here to relax."

Wayne patted her hand tenderly. "That's right, love."

"You say proper markets," said Luke. "What other markets are there?"

"Well, there's the car boots down nearer the coast and ones they call rastros, which are like flea markets. Some places have them every week and others when they have their fairs and fiestas. You get a lot of artisan stuff on those markets, which isn't really our thing."

I noticed a gleam in Luke's eyes and Paul must have too.

"It must be really hard to make a living on those markets," he said.

"Oh, I dunno. You'll not get rich, but if you have a van full of good stuff I reckon you could make a go of it. Depends how strict they are about licences and whatnot though. I guess that varies from place to place."

Luke sat up very straight and his mother's smile was rather taut.

"If you wanted to work those markets, what would you sell?" he asked Wayne.

He chuckled. "Me, I think I'd go for the Del Boy approach. I know that sounds daft, but the thing is you go to those places and you see the same stuff all the time. On the rastros you'll get four jewellery stalls all competing and a few clothes stalls all with the same sort of hippy stuff. On the car boots you mainly get a load of crap that folk cart around every week, but I guess most of them do it for the crack. Yeah, I'd try to find products that were a bit different. I'd buy a few and if they sold, boom!" He slapped the table. "I'd buy a load quick before anyone else could. I reckon I'd have two or three good weeks before the others got onto it, but I'd be looking into something else by then. Yeah, if I had to make a living here that's what I'd do."

"He'd do well too," Kerry said. "He's got markets in the blood."

"You're no slouch either, love."

She shrugged, smiled and sipped her red wine.

Luke was becoming dangerously excited by now, so Paul did his best to quench the fire in his brain.

"Yes, I think someone like you could do it, Wayne. You've got money behind you and if one product failed you'd move onto the next and pretty soon you'd make a killing."

Wayne nodded and pulled his beard, so Luke stroked his.

"But imagine if someone who hasn't got much cash buys an old van and invests in something that ends up not selling." He glanced at Luke. "He'd be ruined straight away."

Linda grunted. "Yes if he or *she* were really stupid that could happen, but like Wayne said, it's about trying things out and only buying a lot if they sell. That way you could afford to have a few failures before you find your killer product."

Luke smiled gratefully, but Paul wasn't done.

"All right, but you still need a fair bit of capital. If this hypothetical person does run out of money he or she will have to beg or borrow some more, probably from his nearest and dearest. Has that not occurred to you, Linda, dear?"

Wayne and Kerry's amused eyes focussed on Linda.

She smiled coldly. "Yes, Paul, dear, but I'm sure that his or her loved ones would be prepared to back him or her if they saw that he or she was determined to make a go of it and had had at least a little success initially."

"Yes, his or her *immediate* family could do that, I guess."

"That's what I meant."

"It wouldn't be easy," I chipped in.

Luke's forefinger shot out across the table. "No, not easy, but I'm sure that he or she could get things off the ground with as little as… four thousand euros."

Paul groaned.

Wayne chuckled. "Thinking of giving it a go, are you?"

"Well, Wayne, I've been racking my brains for ages, and–"

"For a week," Paul interjected.

"And I haven't come up with a better idea yet. I need some wheels anyway, as they've only got one car between them, so if I can pick up an old van I could look into the markets and if it's no go the van'll come in handy anyway."

"Van, tax, insurance, and MOT or whatever they call it here," Paul droned, counting them off on his fingers.

"ITV," said Linda. "You have a look at vans, Luke, and see how much they are."

Paul chuckled. "Bill's ears'll be burning, wherever he is."

"But we're not talking about him," I said.

"They'll still be burning, believe me."

Linda frowned. "One measly text I've had from him, telling me next to nothing."

"Dad'll be fine. So, Wayne, what sort of thing do you think I should sell first?"

He turned to Kerry. "What do you reckon, love?"

"Some little gadget would be a good bet, I think. Yes, some little thing that hasn't been seen much."

"Yeah, something that folk'll see and say, ooh, I need one of them," said Wayne.

"Like what?" said the sceptic.

"Dunno," Wayne said. "If I was you, Luke, I'd go to the rastros and see what's selling. Get online and google around a bit as well. Go on EBay and sites like that and see what's new."

"But it doesn't have to be a gadget, does it?" I said.

"No, but it has to be small and light 'cause of the carriage. Something cheap that you can sell a lot of." Wayne turned to Luke. "What you do is this. You buy a few of whatever you decide and try them out. If they sell you buy in bulk from the Chinese warehouses in England, or here if you can find them. It takes too long for stuff to arrive from China, you see, and they might hammer you in customs."

Luke smiled, then frowned. "Hmm, but it doesn't seem very ethical to just import stuff like that."

Wayne looked puzzled. "Ethical? Worry about being ethical when you're up and running, mate. Suss out the markets and get yourself known first. When you've got a good van and twenty grand in the bank you can start thinking about being ethical, if that's what floats your boat."

"We do try to be ethical when we can though," said Kerry. "We stock some fair trade stuff if the price is right. Some folk like it."

Luke was rubbing his temples. "Oh, such a lot to think about. Thanks for the advice. I'm going to get a van next week and visit the markets I might be able to sell at."

"You'll end up skint," Paul murmured.

"No he won't," said Linda.

"Anyone for afters?" I said. "We've made a Crema Catalana, we hope."

Despite overdoing the cinnamon, the creamy dessert was edible and we soon adjourned to the easy chairs with our coffee and liqueurs. Although it was quite cold and we'd lit the wood-burning stove, Luke managed to lure Wayne out onto the patio and they spent some time there.

Linda glanced towards the door. "There'll be bits of brain all over the place."

Kerry gasped. "What?"

"She means that Luke's fond of picking brains," I explained.

She laughed. "Well Wayne won't mind, and I think we've been to most of the markets around here. He can't stay away from them."

"Luke'll be skint in a fortnight," said Paul.

"No he won't. You underestimate him," said Linda.

"Don't start again, you two," I said.

When the two men finally came inside Luke was beaming.

"Wayne's going to send me some micro houses."

"What are they?" I asked, envisioning camping pods or something of that ilk.

Linda's lovely tan appeared to fade slightly.

Paul would have made a sarcastic comment had the benefactor not been Wayne.

Kerry chuckled. "They're little plastic houses about two inches square that some poor pal of Wayne unloaded on him."

He cringed. "I bought them to help him out of a spot. Two hundred of the damn things. The idea is that you make a little scene with micro houses on micro grass with micro trees, hills and whatnot. I think they make posh ones too, but these are a bit crap."

"Why on earth would anyone want to buy them?" Paul asked him.

Wayne shrugged his huge shoulders. "Dunno, really. I guess it's the same sort of thing as doll's houses, except outdoors, and smaller. In Liverpool folk just laughed at them, so they were back in the van double-quick, but I reckon your retired expats here who've got nowt to do with themselves might buy them." He looked at Luke. "I'd sell them along with the bits of grass and trees and stuff so they can see what a lovely scene they'll make." He chuckled. "I was gonna bring them next time and make a gift of them, but our man here's keen to start and wants to pay me, so they'll be fifty-pee a throw plus carriage."

"How many are there?" Paul asked.

"Er, about 195 I think."

"I've never seen them. They might be really new in Spain," I said with my habitual optimism.

Wayne shrugged. "Should sell for at least a couple of euros apiece. If they don't we'll put it down to experience, eh, Luke?"

"I will, but I'll pay you for them now. I reckon I can sell them, so I want to put my money where my mouth is. When are you going back?"

"Luke! Don't wish our friends away just so you can get these little houses," said Linda.

"Micro houses, Mum. The new craze about to sweep the Alicante hills… and coast."

Wayne sipped his whisky and laughed. "If you come to Liverpool I'll take you on. I think you've got the gift."

"There you go, Luke, a job opportunity," Paul said eagerly.

I noticed that Wayne's face didn't fall.

Luke smiled. "You know, I've done loads of jobs, but I've never really sold anything before. It'll be a totally new challenge."

"If you can flog those daft little things you can flog anything," said Kerry. "I'll send an email tomorrow and they'll be winging their way towards you next week."

"Thanks, and I'll order some micro grass and things to make nice little displays." He pointed to a table by the wall. "A micro hamlet would look lovely there, wouldn't it?"

"No," said Paul. "Dent pullers."

Ten eyes turned towards him.

He shrugged. "I've just been doing a bit of brainstorming. Those little magnetic dent pullers, for getting dents out of cars, is just the sort of thing that blokes'll see and think, ooh, one of those would be handy, even though they'll never need it and if they did it probably wouldn't work."

"Yep, that's the idea, Paul," said Wayne. "Folk go to these rastros and car boots and wander around, but they always like to buy something, just to justify the time they've wasted there."

"I'll look into them," said Luke, looking drunk on water and ideas.

"Like I say, buy a few and try them out," said Wayne. "Though to be honest I reckon a dozen dent pullers will be enough, but you have to have a bit of variety on your stall."

Linda seemed happy that her son now had something to get his teeth into, but she steered the conversation onto other matters and we agreed to meet up for a short walk on Thursday, to see the spot where Aunt Jean had painted from, before lunching in the bar.

"Bill had better be back by then," she said. "His week's up on Wednesday."

A while later Kerry and Wayne thanked us for a lovely evening and departed. Luke made a beeline for the laptop, while his tired and slightly tipsy elders made for their beds.

"What's the worst that could happen?" I asked Paul regarding Luke's new plan.

"He could end up skint and on our hands forever."

"Rubbish. Look, we expected him to arrive practically penniless, so the situation's better than it might have been."

He yawned. "I suppose I'd better look at vans with him, unless Bill gets back in time to prevent a rash purchase."

"I wish he'd ring Linda and put her mind at ease."

"They'll be dancing with wolves now and, baying at the moon."

"Will there be wolves there?"

"Bound to be. Night, love."

# 13

Bill finally called on Sunday evening and told Linda that after two nights' camping they had returned to Riópar and booked into the same cheap hotel they'd stayed at on their first night.

"I thought they were going to head somewhere else," I said.

"Hmm, that's what I said, but he told me it was so nice around there that they didn't see any point in moving on." She frowned. "He says everything's fine, but I've got a feeling that he's a bit fed up of it already."

"It must be cold camping out up there. It'll be December soon."

"Yes, he said it was cold at night and that they got a bit wet, so it might just be that."

"What else could it be?"

"Oh, I don't know, but it was when I asked about Alberto that he started sounding glum. I don't think they're getting on as well as he expected." She smiled. "Maybe he'll cheer up now they've got a roof over their heads."

"When are they coming back?"

"On Wednesday at the latest, he says." She chuckled. "I told him about Luke's market project and he said to tell him not to do anything till he gets back."

"It's a bit late for that. He's already ordered some micro landscape."

"I know. At least it's cheap. He's going to Alcoy with Paul to look at vans tomorrow. Bill's not very mechanically minded anyway. Oh, I'll be glad when he gets back."

"No disasters so far though, touch wood."

We tapped the kitchen table.

"I've had a thought about our trip," I said, as we'd already decided we deserved one at some point.

"Go on."

"We could ask Ana if she wants to come."

"Hmm, could do."

"Then we wouldn't just be a pair of guiris traipsing around. We'd speak more Spanish too."

"Or Spanglish, but yes, we could ask her next Wednesday. She's working this week."

After visiting several second-hand car dealers in and around Alcoy, Luke settled for a sixteen-year-old Fiat Scudo van with a mere 212,000 kilometres on the clock. The next day he drove it home and proudly extolled its suitability.

"It's big enough, but not too big, and the carpet in the back'll be handy if I have to kip in it."

"Why on earth would you do that?" his mother asked.

"To keep costs down, Mum. I plan to go from market to market, touting my wares, and as most are near the coast I can't be driving all the way back every night, can I?"

Paul smiled. "Very true."

"This side door's handy too, so I can whip it open and show my tiny houses in village squares and wherever else I stop."

"I thought they were called micro houses," said Paul.

"They are, but I've realised that there are also micro houses that you can live in, so I've christened mine tiny houses. It'll avoid confusion." He patted the bonnet. "Yep, this is just the job to launch my new career."

In short, one might have thought it was the van of his dreams rather than a rusty, dented, off-white heap that sounded like a tractor with indigestion, but Paul assured us that it was mechanically sound and relatively good value for €1150.

"You could have spent a bit more," Linda grumbled. "We'd have helped you out."

"No, Mum, this is my venture and I can't accept hand-outs."

"It wouldn't be the first," Paul muttered.

"And like Paul says, even if you spend twice that amount you're still getting a pretty old van that might break down. Besides, I want to look the part."

"What part?" I asked.

"The struggling market trader, striving to make ends meet and feed his three little kids."

"What?" Linda and I said at the same time.

He laughed. "Oh, I'm just preparing my patter, which I'll vary according to circumstances."

"Is it insured?" Linda asked.

"Of course it is. I sorted that out yesterday. Yep, on Thursday I'm off to Benidorm. There's a rastro near there that I want to take a look at." He sighed. "Shame the tiny houses won't have arrived."

"Just go and have a look and see if the van gets you there and back," I said.

"Hey, you haven't got anything to sell, have you?"

Paul shook his head. "Afraid not. We haven't had time to accumulate any junk yet. Have you ordered the dent pullers?"

"Yep, just a dozen, like Wayne said. I bought some sticky dashboard pads from the same place near London while I was at it."

"What are they for?" Linda asked.

He grinned. "They're magnetic. You can stick coins and pens and phones to them. Every car should have one. I've ordered some self-watering bulbs too."

"Some what watering whats?" Linda said.

"Self-watering bulbs. They're plastic bulbs with a stem. You stick them in the plant pot and they water slowly for about a week, or they're supposed to. Every plant should have one. I bought a hundred at eighty-pee apiece." He frowned. "Plus postage. I'll have to find a Spanish supplier soon."

I smiled encouragingly. "You know, if I were wandering around a market I might buy a couple of those if they were cheap. They're just the sort of thing that you buy then never use."

"Yep, that's what I thought. The perfect product for a woman whose husband's just bought a dent puller."

"What else have you bought?" Linda asked.

"That's it for now. I've seen some good banana slicers, but I'm going to hang fire for a while."

"Who'd want one of those?" Paul asked.

"Have you never peeled a banana and then thought, ooh, I could just do with slicing it into little bits to make it easier to eat?"

"No."

He laughed and slapped the roof of the van. "Ha, me neither, but some folk are daft enough to buy them."

"What about mobile phone covers?" I said. "Lots of people buy those."

Luke tutted and shook his head. "No, no, no. Wayne warned me off things like that. Too obvious. You get market stalls full of them, he says. No, it's all about thinking outside the box."

"Boxes," said Paul.

"What about them?" I asked.

"Little wooden boxes that people buy to put things in and then never do."

"Cheers, Paul, I'll look into them. Who wants to come for a spin? There's three seats up front."

We all found that we had things to do.

Bill called on Tuesday evening at about half past nine and as Linda was upstairs I answered her phone.

"Hello, Bill."

"Hello, Sue. Do you think Paul could pick me up from Játiva train station?"

"What are you doing there?"

"I've just got off a train."

"Oh, did the jeep break down after all?"

"No, I'm on my own."

"Oh, right. What's happened?"

He sighed. "It's a long story, Sue."

"Hang on, I'll just tell him."

So it was that Paul drove the thirty miles north to the town of Játiva and returned with a weary Bill as the clock neared midnight. Linda and I had been speculating on the nature of his and Alberto's separation and were both eager to interrogate him, but he looked so downcast that Paul and I decided to retire and leave them to it. Paul related Bill's tale of woe to me quietly in bed.

"Are you lying comfortably?" he began.

"Yes."

He sniggered. "Do you want me to jump to the final falling out or start at the beginning?"

I yawned. "Tell me the whole story."

"Well, they left here and drove for a couple of hours until they reached a place called Hellín. They had some elevenses there and Alberto seemed to be in no hurry to press on. When they finally left he drove back the way they'd come for a couple of miles and pulled up outside this blue building set back from the road in the middle of nowhere." He leant on his elbow and grinned at me. "He'd been killing time, you see, though Bill didn't realise that until this afternoon."

"I'm intrigued. Do go on."

"Anyway, this building was some kind of club and Alberto went to knock on the door, as he said a friend of his lived there and he just wanted to say hello. He knocked for ages before a bloke came to the door and they talked for a while. Bill saw the man shake his head and shut the door, but Alberto came back to the van looking happy enough and said that his friend still lived there and they could call in on the way back."

"His friend lives in a club?"

Paul sniggered. "No questions, please, or you'll spoil it. So, they carried on to Riópar which is quite a touristy place because of the source of some river or other, but it's quiet at this time of year. They stayed in a hotel that night and had a skinful, before driving out the next day to have a look at the source of the river. Then they headed off into the forest to camp miles from anywhere. They had a good day rambling around, then Alberto made a campfire and they roasted some meat and sat around in the evening, getting another skinful, but don't tell Linda I've told you this."

"All right. Go on."

"What day was I on?"

"Er, we're up to Friday night, getting our second skinful."

"That's right, so on Saturday they went off to walk a bit more. Bill had a terrible hangover, but Alberto got rid of his by taking nips from this big flask of brandy, so when they got back Bill had to make the fire as Alberto was well on the way to getting his third skinful, ha ha."

"Keep your voice down."

"Sorry, so, Saturday night was more of the same, except it started to rain so they ended up in the tent, supping away. They both had such bad hangovers on Sunday and Alberto's old canvas tent was so wet that they walked back to the car and drove into town. They checked back into the hotel and Alberto was really on a roll by then, annoying everyone with his stories and drinking like a Cossack. By Monday Bill was fed up of him, so he went off walking while Alberto stayed in the bars all day. Bill saw that they really had to get back the next day, so after trying to keep Alberto out of trouble they spent the night and got up late, Bill without a hangover and Alberto still pissed from the night before. Bill couldn't budge him till about three and insisted on driving, so they set off. That's when Alberto started going on about his friend in the place back in Hellín, and that they simply had to drop in to see her." He grinned and paused for effect.

"Come on, what happened next?"

"Well, they get to this club at about five and there's a few cars around, so they go in and, lo and behold, it's like a nightclub with blokes sat up at the bar and half-naked women wandering around."

"At five in the afternoon?"

"Yep, he reckoned they'd just opened and that the blokes had dropped in after a good lunch. Anyway, it turns out that Alberto's friend is this chubby Brazilian woman in her thirties and she's soon up at the bar with them, flirting like mad with Alberto and saying how much she's missed him. One of the last things Alberto said to Bill was that she used to work in a club near Albaida, not far from here, and that they became really good friends there."

"Am I right in thinking that this place was a brothel?"

"Yep, Bill said it was all right though."

"All right?" I gasped.

"Yeah, he said he just had a very dear glass of coke and the girls sort of passed by and asked him if he wanted to go upstairs with them. He said no, of course, and the other blokes there didn't seem in any hurry either. In fact it was with two of them that he got a lift to Albacete."

"Albacete? Isn't that a city?"

"Yes, and he got to the station in the nick of time, otherwise he'd have had to stay there tonight. Alberto did go upstairs with his friend, you see, saying he wouldn't be long, but as Bill sat there he realised that his supposed pal had treated him pretty badly. He got chatting to one of the blokes, who spoke English, and he said he was a businessman and the other chap his client. The client didn't fancy going upstairs and they were heading back to town, so on the spur of the moment Bill decided to go with them. He got his rucksack, left the jeep keys with the barman, and hopped it. How's that for a story to tell his grandkids, eh?"

I sniffed. "A most unsuitable one."

He chuckled. "I wonder if he'll tell Linda the truth."

"Of course he will, if he's got nothing to hide."

Just then we heard hoots of female laughter from downstairs, so we concluded that Linda had taken Bill's account fairly well.

"I wonder if stuff like that will happen to me and Alain in Morocco."

I couldn't help laughing. "Alain doesn't seem the type. Alberto does though. God knows what he got up to on his globetrotting trips."

"Yeah, I wonder, and I wonder if Bill will kick the fat boring git into touch now."

"I thought you didn't mind him."

"I didn't, I just stayed clear of him. He talks too much for me. Linda was right about him being a lush."

"And Rik about him being a good-for-nothing. Oh, Rik and Anke should be back soon. We'll invite them to dinner."

We kissed goodnight and I turned out the light.

# 14

The following day Bill was philosophical about his trip, but said that he was in no hurry to see Alberto.

"He led me on and made me drink too much," he said at breakfast.

"You poor, helpless boy," Linda purred.

Luke chucked. "I'm *appalled* by your behaviour, Dad."

"And that business with his *friend* was the last straw. If he'd been straight and just told me what he wanted to do I wouldn't have minded waiting around for an hour or so."

"In the jeep?" I asked.

"Well, no, at the bar. I am a man of the world, after all, and the girls seemed happy enough, if a little sleepy."

"It can't be much of a life," said Linda. "Though I suppose they're better off there than on the streets."

"They must be sleazy places," said Luke. "I shan't be going no matter how much I earn. I'd never pay for it anyway."

I cleared my throat. "Can we change the subject, please? I'm trying to eat my cereals."

"How much do you weigh now, Bill?" Paul asked him.

He frowned. "Over eighty-two, despite the walking and the hardship. No toast for me today."

"Will you call Alberto?" I asked.

"No, and even if he apologises I shan't be seeing him for a while. He's a bad influence and I must have heard all his stories at least three times already. I shall concentrate on my studies and walk alone."

"You can come walking with us," I said.

"Yes, I may do that."

Little more was said about Bill's escapade and Alberto didn't call, perhaps feeling that Bill was in the wrong for abandoning him. Linda and I were more than happy not to see or hear about him until the pool opened in June, assuming he'd be running it again.

That evening Luke spent a long time in the bathroom and eventually emerged without his beard. His lower face was quite white, but he looked younger and more handsome.

"I'm going for the fresh-faced approach, you see, as opposed to the grizzled trader," he told us over dinner.

"Yes, you looked like a Canadian fur trapper," said his father.

"I'll be off at six tomorrow, but I'll be quiet."

"So early?" Paul said, impressed by his zeal.

"Yep, I've read that to get a stall at this Cisne market near Benidorm you have to be there by seven. It supposed to be quieter on Thursdays and Saturdays than Sundays, but on Sunday I reckon I'll check out the one near La Nucia instead."

"But you won't need a stall, as you've got nothing to sell," said Linda. "Or have you?"

"No, but I'm treating it as a rehearsal. I'll pick folk's brains before they get busy. I was thinking of staying down there too. Can I borrow your sleeping bag, Dad?"

"It's yours. Take the foam mat too. I've no intention of using them again."

"Thanks."

"Never say never, Bill," said Paul.

He shrugged and buttered a slice of toast.

Later on Wayne and Kerry took Linda and I to see the wooded ridge where Aunt Jean had often painted, about a mile to the west the village. We agreed that it was a fitting spot to scatter her ashes, but decided to wait for a significant day before doing so. The six of us had lunch in the bar before saying goodbye until their next trip. I'd got over my snobbishness by then and Linda no longer suspected them of having underworld connections.

Anke and Rik returned on Friday and came to dinner on Saturday. Rik was extremely tanned – almost frazzled, in fact – and declared that he'd finally retired.

"Ha," said Anke.

"I mean it this time. Nigeria was awful, as always. You stay in good hotels but see poverty close by. Why do we need more money when these people have so little, I say? Now I stay here with my Anke and use the damn expensive camera I bought."

"I can show you some scenic places around here," said Bill, now viewing Rik's contempt for Alberto in a new light, I deduced. "We can walk to them whenever you want."

"Yes, that would be good. I need to exercise too. So where is this son of yours?"

"Still on the coast, visiting markets and sleeping in his van, we think," said Linda.

"Ha, an intrepid trader!"

Yes, except that he's got nothing to sell yet. Some of his stuff has arrived too. I hope he'll be back tomorrow."

"He *had* nothing to sell, Linda," said Paul with a smile. "But he has money in his pocket."

"Do you think he'll have bought things to sell?" I asked.

He shrugged. "Tomorrow we'll find out, I expect."

We told them about the products he'd ordered and they laughed.

"This is a good idea, I think," said Rik. "Something curious for people to buy. Nowadays people only want to buy, buy, buy. In Nigeria it's the same. People are poorer, but they all want motorbikes and cars and mobile phones. One day from the dredger I saw two men fighting over a big old mobile phone, really fighting, and I said to my foreman Chinua…" and he was off, telling another interminable tale while Anke looked smilingly on. Over coffee he got Bill alone and droned on about dredging, but he proved to be an attentive audience and Paul later said that he suspected he'd already found an Alberto substitute.

"Bill's the only big talker I know who's also a good listener," I said to Paul later.

"Rik's a bit of a bore, but Bill's better off with him than that drunken slob."

"The best thing about Alberto was that he was Spanish," I said, inadvertently consigning him to history. "You haven't got any Spanish friends yet."

"Well, I've got Alain. He's a bit exotic and speaks good Spanish. He'll have to do for now."

"We're going to ask Ana if she wants to come on a trip with us."

"What kind of trip? Camping, boozing and sex?"

"No, hotels, tourism and good food."

"And shopping?"

I shrugged. "Maybe a little."

On Sunday afternoon Luke returned looking happy and smelling faintly of sweat. His facial tan had begun to even itself out and he immediately launched into an account of his endeavours.

"Go and have a shower first," his mother commanded. "Have you eaten?"

"Sort of."

A while later over a bowl of stew he told us that it was easy enough to get a stall on the Thursday Benidorm market and that he needn't go quite so early next time.

"Don't you need a licence or something?" Paul asked.

"No, you just need ten euros. That gets you a space on the edge, as the proper stalls are always taken. There's some good stuff on sale, but a lot of tat too. There are two cheap places to eat and there's live music on some of the time." He smiled and scratched his head. "As soon as I got there I realised I'd forgotten about something important."

"What's that?" I asked.

"A table. I mean, some lowly sellers just use a rug, but to show off my micro hamlets I'll need a table."

"We have none to spare," Paul said promptly.

He smiled. "Don't worry, I've already got one."

"Where from?"

"From another trader, this bloke from Leicester who'd turned up with a load of old stuff from his house." He shook his head. "Poor misguided man. He'd sold hardly anything by about half twelve, so I offered him thirty euros for his old trestle table. He was chuffed to bits and cleared off right away, so I put my stuff on the table and made a few sales before it closed at two."

"What stuff?" Linda asked.

Paul gazed around the sitting room to see if anything was missing.

Luke chuckled. "Well, by about eleven I'd seen everything and I was itching to go back on Saturday to have a go at selling, so I bided my time and had a bite to eat, then I went to this crummy stall where this Welsh chap had a load of old stuff like metal ornaments, ashtrays, candlesticks, coins and whatnot. I looked at the prices and made some quick calculations and offered him seventy euros for everything except a few breakable things I didn't want. He'd been sat there like a waxwork, but he perked up then and I ended up giving him eighty, as I'd expected, so I shoved it all in a couple of bags and headed off to buy the table."

"Er, I can see just one slight flaw in this spirited purchase, Son," said Bill.

"What's that, Dad?"

"That if the Welshman lacked the… wizardry to sell his goods, why should you be able to do any better?"

"You've taken the words out of my mouth," said Paul.

"Well, by two I'd sold two little metal cannons, a naff brass candlestick, a cute tin cat, an old tobacco tin and a couple more things."

"How much for?" I asked.

"Thirty-four euros," he said proudly. "Mostly to Spaniards too. The thing is the Welshman just sat there looking glum, while I was on my feet collaring everyone who came by." He stretched his arms and sighed contentedly. "That's when I realised I've got a talent for sales."

"Er, what proportion of your stock did you sell?" Bill asked.

He pursed his lips. "Hmm, about a quarter, I think, but I sold a lot more on Saturday."

"How much have you made?" Linda asked.

"Ninety-eight, so I'm already eighteen up, minus the ten for the stall."

"Minus diesel and other costs," said Paul.

"Well, I was just practising really. Today I just walked round the Polop rastro sussing it out. It's more like a car boot sale there, with less proper stalls, so it should suit me just fine."

"I think your tiny houses have arrived from Liverpool," I said.

He leapt to his feet.

"Just a minute," said Linda.

He sat down.

"You appear to have missed Friday out of your itinerary."

"Ah, well, there wasn't a rastro nearby on Friday, so I drove down to the beach at a place called Albir and just chilled out there." His smile suggested he had more to tell.

I had an inkling what it might be, so I asked him if it hadn't been tiresome to spend three nights in the van.

"Ah, well, on Saturday evening I got chatting to a charming lady from Leeds who has an apartment there and she kindly invited me to stay."

Linda screwed up her nose. "What, smelling like you did when you got home today?"

"Not that bad, and I had a shower there. I'll take a change of clothes next week."

"Was she a nice bit of stuff?" Paul asked.

"She was quite a big bit of stuff actually, and no longer young, but very hospitable."

"I don't think we need to go there, Luke," said Linda. "Off you go to play with your mini houses now."

"Tiny houses, Mum."


On Wednesday afternoon in the bar Linda broached the subject of going on a trip with Ana.

(The language the person isn't supposed to be speaking is in italics.)

"Ana, Sue and I want to go on a trip," she said in Spanish.

"Muy bien, Linda."

"Sí. Do you want to come on a trip with us?"

She smiled. "Me? Well, what kind of trip?"

"We aren't sure. Maybe to a city or maybe to the country. In winter it is cold, so maybe a city is better," I said, having prepared the spiel along with my sister.

"Yes, because I don't like the cold."

"We know," said Linda.

"This year I have no holidays left, but in the new year I can take a few days off," she said slowly.

"Bien. Where would you like that we go?" Linda said.

Ana then switched to English, as we no longer stuck to the fifty/fifty rule and launched into our student language whenever the mood took us. "In winter I think south. Yes, south, so really Andalucía, unless you like to come to Murcia to meet with my family."

"One day we'd like to go to Murcia with you, Ana, but first we'd like to take a trip somewhere else," I said, as Linda and I thought more bonding and Spanish studies ought to take place before embarking on such a challenging encounter, as Ana's extended family appeared to be endless.

"OK, yes, a trip. So, we have Granada, a marvellous city with the Alhambra and *Albaicín neighbourhood* and *churches* and many shops and restaurants, but, oh, very cold in winter. Also there is Córdoba, with the marvellous *mosque*, but far from sea, so also maybe cold. Also there is Málaga, pretty city by sea with *fort* and *Roman amphitheatre* and *bullring* and *museums* and *parador hotel* and also many shops and good eating."

"Roman amphitheatre, museums..." I began, but in vain.

"Yes, also there is Almería, easy go there down coast from Murcia. There is giant *Moorish fortress* and ... well, the usuals things. Ooh, and *the beach* too if weather nice." She frowned. "But Almería isn't so interested, I think. Also *to the west* there is Cádiz, a very history city, the old part all *on one part of an island with the modern part* also on *island*, but Cádiz far, far away."

"Well..." Linda began.

Ana then shrieked and slapped the table, making us and the few other customers jump. "Oh, I forgetting Sevilla! Oh, Sevilla is the best, so elegant and always sunny with the marvellous *cathedral* and *Giralda bell tower* and the *royal palace* and *the river* and flamenco. Yes, Sevilla is the best, but also far away. Also there is Huelva, but I not know it and I think it no good."

Already tiring of Ana's bilingual babble I made a cunning suggestion. "I would like to go to Granada," I said in Spanish, before glancing at Linda and subtly twitching my eyebrows to indicate there was a good reason for my choice.

"Oh, but it's too cold for me in winter," Ana said in fluent Spanish.

"I am very keen to see the Alhambra. We can go in March, perhaps."

"No, April or even May, Sue. Granada's very cold."

"All right, so perhaps we can go for a little trip before then. Linda and I don't know Valencia... *yet*."

"We can visit Valencia in one day," said Linda.

"Claro, just a day trip," said Ana.

"That is settled then," I said in English, having no idea how to say it in Spanish.

"OK, Valencia good for me. Now I tell you fun story me happen in the hotel last week..."

When our 'class' was over and we'd walked Ana to her car, Linda guessed that my insistence on visiting Granada was due to an attack of cold feet regarding an extended trip with her.

"Right first time." I sighed. "It'd be too much spending three or four days with Ana now. Let's face it, our classes are a bit of a joke and I don't think I could keep it up for more than a day. We need to improve our Spanish before we go anywhere with her for longer."

On arriving home we were still discussing this weighty matter.

"So," said Bill, ensconced in an armchair with a book. "Am I to understand that you propose to carry out a linguistic *coup d'état* before taking a lengthy trip with your friend, or might *coup de grâce* be the more appropriate term?"

"If you mean that we want our Spanish to be better than Ana's English, then yes," Linda said.

"We'll need a proper teacher to achieve that," I said. "Someone who'll really test us and give us lots of homework."

"Were you to contract such a teacher, I'd quite like to take part in the classes too," Bill said.

"But you don't speak any Spanish," Linda said in Spanish.

He smiled tightly. "But… I… know… considerably… more Spanish… than you… think, señoras."

"Wow, that was right," I said in English.

He shrugged modestly. "I'm making progress, quietly away. Yes, I think a *bona fide* teacher would be a splendid idea. Shall I have a look online and see who's available in the area?"

"Yes," I said.

"But someone who'll come here. We don't want to be traipsing to Alcoy or somewhere," Linda said. "What about Paul?"

"I doubt he'll be up to it, or up for it," I said. "He can sit in if he wants."

In the meantime Lucky Luke had assembled quite a collection of tiny houses and accessories and was raring to go. He'd bought a large water container to drink and occasionally wash from, and also a small gas stove and other items that Alberto had provided on the ill-fated camping trip.

"I'll be totally self-sufficient this time," he said over dinner that evening.

"What about going to the loo?" his mother asked.

"I can pee anywhere and I'll just nip into a bar to do the other."

"Will you have room to sleep with the table and all your stock?" Paul asked.

"Just about. I can shove some of it on the front seats if need be. That's the beauty of my line, you see, that it doesn't take up much space. Hey, I could take one of your Aunt Jean's pictures and try to flog that."

"No way," said Linda. "They're sacred."

"Family heirlooms," I added.

"They're sat there unframed in that studio that's not being used," he said. "It's the best room in the house too, with that big window and good views. It's a shame not to use it."

I shrugged. "It's there to be used, as a studio."

"I might have a go at painting one day," said Linda.

Bill forked a mushroom and waved it. "As one walks before one runs, one must also draw before one paints."

Paul sipped his wine and smiled. "To be honest, you two do need something to do."

"We're always doing something," I said defensively.

"It's true though," said Linda. "We do most of the housework and cooking, and we read and study and walk, but we're not exactly rushed off our feet."

Bill waved another mushroom. "Work, or in this case tasks, expand to fill the time available for their completion. Parkinson's Law."

"Hmm, it's all right in summer when we've got the pool, but I suppose we should be a bit more active and creative really," I conceded.

"You need a hobby," said Paul, reminding me of the day back in spring when Anke had annoyed me by asking solely about our husbands' hobbies.

"I'm going to do some drawing and see how it goes," said Linda.

"Maybe I'll have a go too then," I said weakly.

Linda smiled. "It may be preordained."

"What?"

"That we follow in Aunt Jean's footsteps and make use of her studio. We weren't too bad at drawing when we were youngsters. Bagsy the car tomorrow morning."

"I'm out on the bike with Alain."

"I'm out walking with Rik."

"What for?" I asked her.

"We're going to Alcoy to buy some drawing pads and pencils."

"But there are some in the drawers in the studio."

"All the pads have been used. Besides, Aunt Jean's brilliant sketches will only depress us, and they're family heirlooms too. No, we need to make a fresh start."

"All right, we'll go tomorrow," I said, feigning enthusiasm, as I believed that hobbies embarked on in this spirit were destined to peter out.

Luke, perhaps sensing my feeling of restlessness, suggested that we drive down to La Nucia on Sunday. "Then you can see me in action, unless I've sold everything by then, in which case I'll be home on Saturday."

"I suppose I can have a day off the bike for once," said Paul.

"That's settled then. It'll do you all good to get out and about."

# 15

The following afternoon after an early lunch Linda and I walked to Aunt Jean's favourite drawing and painting spot, pulled our new pads and pencils from my knapsack, and surveyed the views.

"I think I'll have a go at the village," said Linda. "It's got more straight lines."

"I'll try the mountain to the left then," I said, thinking it might be easier.

"Are we supposed to draw standing up?"

I held my A4 pad and poised my pencil. "I don't think so, no."

We then scoured the scrubby clearing surrounded on three sides by pine trees, but only found one rock suitable for sitting on.

"You have a go first," I said. "I'm still getting psyched up."

It was breezy and the temperature was about eleven degrees. Seeing Linda perched on the rock in her coat did little to inspire me, but she produced a sketch that most children would have been proud of, so I took her place, gave my hands a good rub, and set to work.

"Er, would you mind leaving me to it for a while?" I said as she peered over my shoulder at the blank sheet.

She wandered away and I tried my best to reproduce a rocky outcrop skirted by pine trees and cultivated fields lower down the slopes. Twenty minutes later my drawing hand had become rather numb, but I wasn't too distressed by my first effort. I found Linda sitting against a tree, sketching an unprepossessing view of road and fields.

"It's too bloody cold and my bum's wet," she said.

I displayed my open pad. "What do you think of this?"

"Hmm, is it the Cotswolds?"

"Don't be daft."

"No, it's not bad. Not as good as mine, but not bad."

"Yours isn't exactly a Michelangelo, Linda. Where's the perspective on that? The road's supposed to get narrower."

She held up her pencil and looked down the road, then at her pad. "Hmm, I see what you mean. Still, we haven't done too badly for beginners."

"I'm not showing mine to the boys. They'll just laugh."

Linda tore out the two sheets she'd drawn on and crumpled them up. "They're not seeing anything till I've improved, a lot."

I followed suit and we walked briskly home.

That evening we commandeered the laptop and watched a few drawing tutorials on YouTube, before reading several short articles.

"It appears that we have to buy special drawing easels and boards and stands," I said.

"That's the internet for you. Everyone's on the make. Aunt Jean's easel will be fine and there's a sloping board thingy to use at the table."

"It's going to be too cold to draw for long outside."

"Except on really sunny days."

"Do you think we'll get into it and keep it up?" I said.

"I think I will, yes, but I'm not sure if you've got enough talent for it."

"Ha!" I said, injecting considerable scorn into that short word. "We'll see about that."

Over dinner Bill pointed out that the great Alfred Wainwright – who wrote and illustrated many books about the Lake District and other areas of natural beauty – used to draw from the photographs he took on his frequent walking trips.

"Isn't that cheating?" Linda asked.

"It was more practical for him. Besides, as well as the photos he also had the view in his mind's eye. I have several of his books back home." He sighed. "I would dearly like to bring the rest of my library over soon."

"You've got loads of books here," said Linda.

"And about two thousand more at home, dear."

"Feel free to line your study with them," Paul said.

"Our study, but yes, books do furnish a room."

"We haven't spoken about selling our houses and maybe buying another here for a while," I said.

Paul shrugged. "There's no hurry."

"The rent is a handy bit of income for us," said Bill.

"And we're getting on all right, aren't we?" said Linda brightly. "Even with Luke here."

Bill cleared his throat ominously. "Despite being bereft of my books, I'm quite happy as we are. Should one of us, or rather two of us, decide to buy another house they would suddenly have lots of things to occupy their time. They would feel ever so busy and industrious, but I fear it would an illusory industriousness."

Linda sighed. "What are you on about now?"

"Harking back to the subject of occupying ourselves which we discussed yesterday, many people combat their essential aimlessness by buying or building and then furnishing new houses, when what in fact they should do, unless they truly need to move house, is to find worthwhile things to occupy their time."

"People like moving to nicer houses," I said. "In summer we might find we're rather crowded here."

"There's no hurry," Paul repeated, proving Bill's point to some extent, as for him a house move would be a tiresome chore which would interrupt his cycling.

"I can't think about such mundane matters now anyway," said Linda, tilting back her head. "I'm an *artist*, and so is Sue, and us artists live on a higher plain."

"We haven't seen any of your drawings yet," said Paul.

"And you won't until we've done something half decent," I said with a smile, pleased to find myself looking forward to having another go the next day.

"This is precisely what I was referring to the other evening," Bill said on Sunday as we stood among the stalls at the market on the edge of an industrial estate on the outskirts of La Nucia. It was a sunny day and warmer down there, only a few miles from the coast.

"What was that?" I asked.

"That people have nothing meaningful to do. All these elderly foreigners, not to mention the surprising number of Spaniards, probably come here week after week to buy things they don't need."

Linda raised her eyes. "Maybe they just like coming, Bill. It's nice to wander round and there are good views of the mountains, so spare us the philosophy and let's find Luke."

"No, let's look at the stalls first," said Paul. "Once we find him I bet we won't get the chance."

So we toured the market and, lo and behold, we all found something to buy. Linda and I bought some fingerless mitts for our drawing expeditions and she also bought a green beret which she intended to wear while on the job.

"It looks a bit silly," said Bill.

By way of reply she pulled it on.

Paul bought a scraper which he planned to use on the wooden door and window blinds when he finally got around to revarnishing them, while among the piles of books Bill found a tatty Wainwright volume which he presented to us, 'for inspiration', he said.

"He used an awful lot of lines and dots," Linda said on perusing a sketch of a mountain as we strolled along. "It must have taken him ages."

"We'll compare his style to others," I said, a little overwhelmed by his detailed approach.

She tilted her beret. "Yes, I think I'll be more minimalist than him."

"I spy something beginning with L," said Paul, and sure enough, right on the edge of the market, there was Luke, sitting behind his table on a camping chair, but not for long, because when an elderly couple strolled past he was on his feet, smiling, talking and gesticulating.

We closed in a little and saw him demonstrating the versatility of his micro hamlet, by substituting one house for another and moving the trees around. While the woman paid close attention, the man began to peruse the other objects on the rather crowded table.

"I think he's picked up a dent puller," Linda murmured.

Just then the lady shook her head, so he produced a real live plant from under the table and jabbed a self-watering bulb into the soil, before enthusiastically explaining how it worked. She nodded and prodded it, but they soon walked away without buying anything.

"Damn time-wasters," Linda snapped. "After all that effort."

Luke didn't seem too put out and when he saw us he beckoned us over. Linda attempted to accost him behind the table, but he shooed her away and immediately launched into his spiel, punctuated by whispered instructions. For the latter I will resort once more to italics.

"So, ladies and gentlemen, what you see here are the finest tiny houses on the market, and I don't just mean this market, ha ha. *Mum, pick one up and look at it.* These idyllic scenes are all the rage in Scandinavia right now. *Sue, take that spare hillock.* And are just the thing to brighten up the corner of a room. *Paul, stop frowning.* You can go for the winter chalet scene and sprinkle artificial snow on the durable micro grass, or…" He quickly changed the chalets for cottages. "…if you prefer a rustic scene you can have these cute little cottages. *Dad, get your wallet out.* My stock is running low, so grab a bargain before they all go." He gazed beyond us and sighed. "Relax, there's no-one looking."

Linda tutted. "You poor boy, is no-one buying anything?"

"I've done all right actually. What's that on your head?"

"My artist's beret. Linda and me are both budding artists now. We've been out drawing three times already. Ooh, is that chair for sale? We could do with a couple of those. Sue feels silly carting the easel through the village."

"No, Mum, I've only just bought it, but I can show you the stall." He looked at his watch. "You know what? Seeing as you're here I think I'll call it a day. You can give me a hand with the stuff, then there's someone I want you to meet."

On the way to the van Luke told us that he'd made €164 over three days, minus the €30 for the stalls.

"Have you subtracted the cost price of the goods?" Paul asked.

"Er, no, but it's not that much. I've sold mainly single tiny houses. God knows what they want one for, but they might be back for more if they get to like the daft little things. The self-watering bulbs are a bit of a flop, but it is winter. I've sold seven dent-pullers though, but I think the sticky dashboard pads are old hat. Other stalls have them too."

Linda peered into the back of the van as Luke filled it.

She sniffed. "How many nights have you slept in here this week?"

"Three, I'm afraid, down near the beach."

"Is that allowed?" Paul asked.

"No, but it's just a van. When I'm ready for bed I dive in and no-one knows I'm there."

Linda frowned. "It seems like a poor sort of way for an educated man to live."

"Oh, it's just a bit of a lark and it gets me out of the house."

"That's true," said Paul, as I knew he would.

"And I'm learning new things. You can't learn enough new things."

I expressed my agreement with this, as I was enjoying my drawing more than I'd expected and, between you and me, making better progress than my sister, though I refrained from rubbing this in.

After we'd bought two cheap looking camping chairs, Luke led us through the busier stalls and stopped beside a large, covered one selling all kinds of leather goods.

"Don't stare, because it's early days." he whispered.

"Who are we not staring at?" Linda asked.

"Who do you think? Just browse and pretend you don't know me."

"But I thought we were meeting someone."

"Only if you take that silly beret off."

She snorted and pocketed it.

I stepped aside from this scene of gentle bickering and saw a slim young woman with olive skin and long black hair behind the tables. The only other person there was a calm, portly man of about fifty, so I was quick to deduce that the woman – in her mid-twenties and dressed in a black t-shirt and blue jeans – was the object of Luke's desire, as she was extremely pretty. I took the man to be her father. There were a few people milling around, but when she saw Luke she smiled and approached us.

He introduced us quickly in Spanish and she said she was pleased to meet us.

"This is Sara. She is my friend and is teaching me things about the markets," he told us in slow Spanish.

"What… you think of Luke… products, Sara?" Linda asked her.

She giggled. "Muy diversos. Oh, discúlpenme," she said, and went to attend a customer.

"Come on," said Luke, hustling us away. "There's a cafe over there."

Both Paul and Bill glanced back to take a final look at the lovely girl, while Linda launched a quick-fire interrogation.

"Is she a gypsy?"

"No."

"Is that her father?"

"No."

"Is he her… husband?"

"No."

"Do they live in a van?"

"No. Shush, Mum, I'll tell you about her when we get a drink. I'm parched."

It transpired that Sara was twenty-three and a native of Malaga, thus the dark hair and skin. Having failed to find a suitable job after doing a degree in business studies in Madrid, the previous summer she'd joined her uncle, something of a black sheep in her affluent family, to get some hands-on business experience on the markets around Alicante, where he'd moved to after divorcing his wife some years earlier. She enjoyed the bustling outdoor life more than she'd expected and was making good money, so she'd stayed on after the summer and had no plans to return home in the immediate future. She lived in her uncle's flat in Sant Vicent del Raspeig, a large town just inland from Alicante, and from there they visited the markets mainly to the north, five or six days a week, in his big Mercedes van.

"That's a relief," Linda said after Luke had filled us in.

"What is?"

"That she's from a respectable family and only working here for a bit of fun, like you."

Luke laughed and shook his head. "You'd be surprised how much money can be made on the markets, Mum. Her uncle's quite well-off and she's doing all right too. After she finished her degree she did two work placements and the only proper job she's been offered was one where she'd have got paid for twenty hours a week and have had to work forty, in Madrid too. That's how bad it is in Spain right now. There are far too many qualified people around."

Bill sipped the first beer he'd been allowed to drink since returning from the camping trip. "So where are you up to with her?"

He smiled. "We're just friends, Dad. We'll remain so until she shows any sign of wanting us to be anything more than that."

"She's rather young," I said.

"All the more reason not to rush her."

"Does she know you're not just a scallywag in an old van?" Linda said.

"Ha, what else am I? Oh, I've told her about my studies and whatnot. As I say, it's early days."

Although it was only one o'clock, he suggested a bite to eat, as at two he was going to help them dismantle the stall.

"What does the uncle think of you?" Paul asked.

"I think he likes me. We're both black sheep, you see. He did all sorts of jobs before he got into the market business. He told me he used to be a heavy drinker and that getting up at four or five in the morning made him knock the nightlife on the head. We've quite a bit in common really. He's called Paco."

After a light lunch we said goodbye to Luke, who expected to return home before dark but in fact got back as we were about to go to bed.

"Paco invited me back to theirs for dinner," he explained.

"Did it go well?" I asked.

"Yes, it was fine. I'm off again on Tuesday to help them at the Altea market."

"Won't you have to order more goods?" said Paul.

He yawned. "Nah, I'm just going to help them on Tuesday and Wednesday. I think I'll run down my micro stock and... well, look into other things. I'm off to bed. Goodnight."

"I think he's already getting cold feet," Paul said after Luke had tramped up the stairs.

Bill chuckled. "I think he's getting his feet under that girl's uncle's table, and from what he's told us he could do worse. I quite fancy Sara."

Linda frowned. "What?"

"As a prospective daughter-in-law, I was about to say."

# 16

As Bill had forgotten to look for a Spanish teacher for us, a few days later Linda and I went online and googled pertinent words and phrases, only in Spanish, as we preferred to find someone who couldn't or wouldn't speak English in class. While it's handy for a language teacher to be able to quickly translate odd words, on the whole it's better if they stick to the language being taught. We weren't having much luck – the nearest available teacher we'd found lived in Onteniente, twenty-odd miles away – and when I returned to the study with two cups of tea my naughty sister had begun to search for art teachers.

"That's not what we're after," I said.

"There is method in my madness," she said dramatically.

"I wouldn't call it madness, Linda, but it'd be a bit self-indulgent to have two teachers coming and going. We are pensioners, after all."

She looked up and grinned. "And what language would a drawing teacher speak, pray?"

"Er, Spanish, if they're Spanish."

She turned back to the screen. "Exactly."

"Ah, you mean that while they're teaching us drawing we pick their brains about Spanish too?"

"Well, we'd speak it and sort of hint that we wouldn't mind if they corrected us now and then." She looked up and grinned again. "Just think, a Spanish person all to ourselves for an hour or more. They won't speak Spanglish like Ana, and they can't rush off like Nieves or Lola or the other people we see around. We'd have a captive audience," she said with a cackle. "All *ours*."

"And have you found anyone?"

"Not yet, but there are more folk who reckon to be art teachers than language teachers."

I sighed. "We might have to stick up another advert."

"Wait, here's a woman in Alcoy who teaches drawing and painting… oh, no, she's called Martine. That's not a Spanish name so she won't do."

"I'm off to draw for a bit," I said, before walking up to the studio where I'd been having a go at sketching from some old photos on Aunt Jean's handy drawing board. I found it very soothing and I'd just outlined the Acropolis when Linda came thundering up the stairs with the open laptop in her arms.

"I've found a candidate, Sue. Look, a chap in Cocentaina called Álvaro is offering drawing and painting classes *a domicilio*. Hmm, domicile. Does that mean his domicile or ours?"

"Well, when you see pizzas or whatnot *a domicilio* it means they deliver them."

"Great!" She clapped her hands together. "That means he'll deliver himself here then. Shall I write and ask him to come?"

"How much does he charge?"

"He doesn't say."

"Is there a telephone number?"

"Yes."

"Hmm, you know, I think it'd be better if you called. If he starts speaking to you in English we won't bother with him."

"Why do I have to call him?"

"Because it's your idea." I smiled. "Unless you don't feel up to it. I suppose he might understand me better."

"Rubbish, I'll call. Hmm, I'd better make some notes first."

Making notes was something we often did when faced with an impending linguistic challenge, but just ten minutes later Linda felt that she had the lexical armoury required for the task. She sent me out of the room, claiming that I made her feel nervous, so I wandered downstairs and told Bill that his wife had overlooked his language needs in favour of a Spanish-speaking drawing teacher.

He shrugged. "Whatever you think best. I'm not too bothered really. I'll plod on with my studies and speak it when I can. Learning Spanish isn't the be-all and end-all, after all."

"Does Rik speak Spanish?"

"Quite a bit." He smiled. "He's going to lend me a camera."

"You've got one."

"Oh, just a little digital one. This is a 35mm Canon. Rik's into developing his own photos, you see. He's got a dark room."

I realised that I'd only ever entered Rik and Anke's house once. "I see."

"He's always snapping away when we're out walking, so I might as well have a go."

I chuckled. "We're all turning into hobbyists."

He shrugged. "C'est la vie for us retired folk, Sue. When I was at the bank I couldn't wait to get home and into my books, but now there are so many hours in the day. Graham Greene once said that he wondered how people who don't do something creative can escape the melancholy of existence, or something along those lines. He was a manic depressive, mind you, but I see his point and I think it applies to all of us."

"Is cycling creative?"

"Hmm, good question. Perhaps when I say creative what I mean is something challenging and fulfilling enough to take us out of ourselves. As Rousseau once said–"

"Sue!" Linda shrieked down the stairs in the nick of time.

"Excuse me, Bill, I think your wife requires me."

He smiled. "Good news, I think."

I trotted upstairs to the studio.

"Álvaro sounds *perfect* for us, Sue. He's only twenty-six and he's got ever such a nice deep voice. He's going to drive over on Monday morning and give us our first class."

"Did he speak English to you?"

"Not a word."

"How much will he charge?"

"Thirty euros for two hours."

"That's OK if he's driving here."

"He sounded surprised when I called and a bit apologetic when he named the price. I've got a feeling he hasn't got all that much work. We'd better get cracking." She opened her pad and placed it on the drawing board.

"What's the hurry?"

"Because he'll want to see our work, of course, and we always throw it away."

"That's true," I lied, as I'd kept a couple of landscapes I was pleased with. "Oh, we're supposed to be meeting Anke for coffee at twelve."

"Oh, you go, then you can use the board later."

"We'll have to buy another one."

"Let's see what Álvaro says first. We might be wasting our time."

I recalled Bill's wise words. "Not if it satisfies our creative urge. See you in a while."

We didn't see Luke until Sunday evening and his neat, cleanly shaven appearance suggested he hadn't been sleeping in the van. He told us that after helping out on the Altea market on Tuesday and the Teulada market on Wednesday he'd ingratiated himself so much with Paco, Sara's uncle, that he'd been invited to stay in his spare room for the rest of the week.

"Did you sell much in Benidorm and La Nucia?" Paul asked.

"Er, well, I didn't actually bother getting a stall this week. I preferred just to help them and learn the tricks of the trade." He smiled. "I'm already getting them more sales from the foreigners."

"Is he paying you?" Paul asked.

He tutted. "No, he offered to slip me some cash, but I refused. I told him I was just doing a work placement like the ones Sara had to do. She laughed at that."

"And Sara?" his mother said, raising her brows.

He assumed a prudish look. "We're still just friends. I think love might well be in the air, but as you can imagine, in a situation like this I have to be on my best behaviour. Paco's not daft, of course, but I think he appreciates my… gentlemanly ways."

"So do you see yourself becoming a real market trader?" I asked.

"I don't see why not. I've got the gift of the gab and it's a damn sight better than a lot of the jobs I've done. Yes, I feel that I've finally landed on my feet. What's new here?"

I told him about our impending drawing class.

"Tomorrow? Oh, good, I'll be here to see how you get on."

"You'll stay out of our way," Linda said. "We want no distractions."

The next morning Álvaro arrived ten minutes early and if there was ever a case of the voice not fitting the man, this was it. His voice was indeed soft and deep, like that of a well-fed baritone, but he was a scrawny, hollow-cheeked lad and very pale for a Spaniard. He appeared to be the epitome of the struggling artist and this proved to be the case, as we quizzed him thoroughly, using our extensive mental notes, in an effort to put off the moment of truth.

He'd studied *Bellas Artes*, or Fine Arts, in Valencia, but hadn't attempted to become a teacher like many of his colleagues, not because the job for life and handsome salary didn't motivate him, but because he thought himself incapable of passing the extremely arduous state exams. Instead he'd returned to the family home to draw, paint and earn a little money by giving classes.

"Do you have many students at the moment?" I asked him.

He smiled shyly. "Only three right now."

Linda smiled. "Well, now you have five."

"No, three including you, if you like my classes." He sighed and pushed back his long dark hair. "Some people don't like them. My other student doesn't like them much, I believe, but she is only fourteen and her parents make her come."

"Oh, does she go to your house?" I asked, as it was my turn.

"Yes. She is my cousin, you see."

We were in the small parlour and Álvaro asked us if we'd be doing the classes there.

"No, we have a studio upstairs," Linda said. "Our aunt was an artist. You can see some of her pictures now."

"That is one on the wall," I said.

"Of this village," said Linda.

He narrowed his dark eyes and nodded. "Very nice, very competent."

"Would you like a drink?" I said.

"A glass of water, please."

"Would you not like some coffee?" Linda said.

"We have made some," I said.

"It is hot," Linda said.

"Yes, please, a little coffee."

I think we peppered him with trivial questions and comments because we were on a language high. The wonderful thing about Álvaro was that we understood almost everything he said first time, because he spoke in such a simple and ponderous way. When he went to use the bathroom Linda said that she didn't mind how bad a drawing teacher he was, as long as he kept on talking and answering our questions.

"I bet he's a good teacher though," I said. "In my experience the unassuming ones are often the best."

"You should know, Miss."

Álvaro liked the studio and made polite comments about Aunt Jean's unframed paintings.

"Do you paint... how do you say paintings of the... countryside? I asked.

"Pintura o cuadro de paisaje, o pintura o cuadro paisajístico," he said slowly.

His painstaking translation caused Linda and I to exchange a gleeful look.

"And do you paint them?" I asked.

"When I was younger, but now I paint more abstract works."

"Did you bring any?" Linda asked.

He blushed slightly. "No." he sipped his coffee. "Shall we begin?"

"Yes. Do you want to see our drawings?" I said, as we'd set aside our very finest works for him to peruse.

"No, that isn't necessary." He took a cheap pad and a packet of pencils from his little knapsack and we ushered him to the prime spot at the drawing board, before sitting down on either side of him.

He rubbed his narrow nose. "I think we will begin with some automatic drawing, er… unless you wish to do something else."

"Ha, you are the teacher," I said.

"What is automatic drawing?" Linda asked with pencil poised.

He smiled weakly. "Well, automatic drawing is supposed to express our subconscious feelings, so we just begin, like this, to draw whatever our brain communicates to our hand. We just draw and try not to think about what it is we are drawing. Please begin to do it too, and we will see what we get."

"That looks like a duck," said Linda.

He smiled and continued to draw. "Please begin."

I obeyed and found myself sketching a mountain outline as I'd done so many times before, while Linda just sat staring at her empty sheet. Left to my own devices I would probably have gone on to draw a conventional landscape, but as Álvaro's pencil was now whizzing all over the place I followed suit and was soon doodling merrily away.

"What is the matter, Linda?" Álvaro said.

"I cannot start. Maybe I don't have a sub… sub…"

"Subconsciente?"

"Sí."

He tittered, dipped his fingers in his coffee, and splattered her sheet. "Now try."

"Ooh, it is easy now," she said as she began to join the splotches. "Why are we doing this, Álvaro?"

"Don't think or speak, Linda."

"Vale."

After about five minutes he told us to put down our pencils. "Sue, what do you see in your drawing?"

I looked at the mass of squiggles. "Er, I don't know."

"Let me see. Yes, this is good. Your mind was free and you allowed your subconscious to decide what to draw."

I'd actually been wondering what possible use the activity could have, but I just nodded.

"Can I see yours Linda?" He took the pad and frowned. "Hmm, a lot of straight lines here."

"I was… connecting the… coffee."

"Yes, perhaps that was a mistake." He licked his lips and gritted his teeth. I saw that his forehead had become moist, despite the coolness of the room.

"Yours has a lot of detail, Álvaro," I said cheerfully, as he reminded me of a student teacher entering the classroom for the first time.

He gazed despondently at the dense doodles. "Yes, I think I was nervous. When I do this at home I draw much less, sometimes almost nothing."

Linda beamed at the poor lad. "What are we going to do next?"

"Well, yes, now, er… let me see." He delved into his bag and pulled out some photos, before selecting one seemingly at random. "This is a bicycle."

"Sí," I said, as there was no mistaking the familiar machine.

"Sue's husband, Paul, he likes to ride his bicycle a lot," Linda said, winking at me.

"Yes, he goes for many kilometres on his bicycle, up hills, and down… hills," I said.

"He… often goes with his friend Alain."

"Alain is French, but he now lives near here."

"Do you ride a bicycle, Álvaro?" Linda asked him.

"Er, no, not now." A bead of sweat trickled down his temple.

"Shall we draw the bicycle, Álvaro?" I said.

"Yes… I mean, no. No, er… please draw the spaces around and within the bicycle."

Linda's face coloured and I knew she was about to burst out laughing, but a sharp glance from me averted this calamity, as Álvaro was so anxious that I feared he might have bolted from the room, never to be seen again.

"When, er… we draw, we should not think about the object we are drawing. Here, er… there is not only a bicycle."

Linda leant over. "No, there is also a tree, here… on the left."

"No, yes, but ignore the tree." He stared at the photo.

I took the liberty of patting his arm. "Please continue, Álvaro."

"Yes, what I mean is, as well as the bicycle there is space. I want you to draw the space, not the bicycle. Let us begin."

Once I'd begun I sort of saw what he meant and strove to concentrate on the spaces between the frame, wheels and so on. The result of my compliance was a very weird looking machine, while Linda's was quite good, because, she later admitted, she'd cheated and drawn the actual bicycle. Álvaro's drawing was an almost perfect reproduction, which restored our confidence in him somewhat.

He held our pads in each hand and nodded. "Good, Linda. Sue, I think you saw too much space or… something." He sipped his cold coffee and gulped. "What would you like to do now?"

"Can we draw a face?" Linda said. "I can never draw a good face."

"A conventional face?"

"Ha, what other…" She felt my glare. "Yes, a conventional face."

He smiled and sighed. "Yes, we can do that."

What followed was a textbook face-drawing tutorial in which he made us draw an egg, four or five times, before we sketched the jawline and then inserted the eyes exactly half way down, followed by the nose, ears, mouth, eyebrows and hair. I had a feeling that his young cousin received classes of this type and we were quite content to draw, scrap and repeat our efforts time and time again, chatting in Spanish all the while. He soon relaxed and towards the end of the class confessed that he'd assumed we'd be more proficient in the basic techniques, as his previous adult students had been, and would wish him to take a more esoteric approach.

"But really, after learning the basic techniques, each artist must follow their own path," he concluded.

I smiled. "I would like to see some of your paintings, Álvaro."

"Well, I can bring a few next time," he said, now confident that there'd be a next time.

"Do you sell many of your paintings?" Linda asked.

He shook his head. "No, I… no, I just draw and paint. One day I may try to have a local exhibition, but…" He smiled and shrugged. "What would you like to do next time?"

"More drawing techniques," I said. "It has been very useful."

"I would like to be able to draw animals," said Linda.

He smiled. "Which animals?"

"First a cat. I like cats. Soon we will have a cat and I would like to draw it."

Neither Bill nor Paul was keen on this idea, partly because it would entail inserting a cat flap, but they knew she'd get her way in the end.

"Yes, we can draw cats, if you like, and any other animals you choose," he said more brightly, perhaps envisioning many stress-free sessions and a little money in his pocket.

Downstairs we introduced him to Luke, who presented him with a sticky dashboard pad. "Surplus stock," he explained.

"It's my mother's car, but no doubt she'll like it, thank you," he said much more quickly than he'd spoken to us, which raised him still more in our estimation.

"He seems a bit shy," Luke said when he'd gone.

"He's just deep, unlike you," his mother said. "He's going to be a brilliant art and Spanish teacher."

"He might not correct us when we venture beyond our script," I said.

She grinned. "I think you'll find that he will."

"Yes, I suppose he will when you tell him to."

# 17

As Christmas approached we were all content with our daily routines. Bill walked and snapped away with Rik, then spent many hours in his darkroom, occasionally bringing home examples of his work.

"They're all right," Linda said on viewing a typical mountain scene. "But I'm sure you'd get better pictures with a good digital camera."

"Nonsense! Clearer, maybe, but these photos have soul, my dear."

"Well I think they're very nice," I said.

"They also *exist*. How many photos do people take on digital cameras that are never printed? We used to cherish our photos. We paid for the film and developing and made albums that we still possess to this day."

Linda snorted. "It's dead easy to make albums nowadays. You just need plenty of paper and ink cartridges, and an album."

"And how many digital photo albums do we have?"

"None," I said, seeing his point.

"I've got trillions of photos," said the belligerent one. "I can make an album any time I like."

"Ha, yes, but I *will* make one, of proper photos, eventually."

"Well, I'm glad you're knocking about with Rik rather than that lousy lush who led you astray," she said, and I had to agree.

"I think Rik really has retired now," Bill said. "And I believe his budding friendship with such a charming, fascinating man has helped to convince him that there's more to life than dredging."

"Who's that then?" Linda said.

Bill just smiled.

Paul cycled with Alain about three times a week and went out for shorter rides most other days. Neither Bill nor Linda could really understand why he found so much cycling so enjoyable.

"If it were me, I think I'd join a club," Linda said one morning while Paul was out on his bike. "He'd get to know more people and speak more Spanish."

"He's not averse to the idea, but he's in no hurry."

"I'd cycle less and do other things," said Bill. "Surely going out twice a week is enough."

"He gets a tremendous buzz from cycling which lasts for ages afterwards."

"Ah, yes, endorphins, a natural type of opioid, not to be confus–"

"So the next day he wants to do the same again. It's about the bikes and the scenery and whooshing down the hills as well, of course, but I think that great feeling's the main thing. I suppose we get it a bit when we do longer walks."

Bill patted his stomach. "I agree, though Rik and I stop a lot to practise our art. I'll crack eighty kilos before Christmas, you'll see."

"Who'll we invite to Christmas dinner?" Linda asked.

"Anke and Rik will be in Holland and I think Alain will be in London. He's about to sell his apartment and wants to settle his affairs."

"His debts," said Linda.

"Yes, and Ana's going to spend a few days in Murcia with her family."

"When are we going for our day trip with her?"

"You suggest it, if you like. To be honest a whole day of Spanglish would be a bit much for me," I said, as I was finding our weekly meetings quite enough.

"Hmm, we'll see. Are Kerry and Wayne coming out?"

"In January, I think."

She stuck out her bottom lip. "It'll just be us four then. Oh, and Luke, of course."

"Will he not be spending Christmas Day with his new family?" I said, as we'd seen very little of him.

"No, they're going to Malaga," said Bill. "I think he's going to celebrate his birthday with them on the 21st, then again with us on Christmas Day."

"What will they do?"

"Go to Benidorm market, then out for lunch, I think."

Linda frowned. "Hey, how come you know so much about our long-lost son?"

"He phoned me earlier. When he needs some advice he knows who to call."

"What advice?"

"Oh, man to man stuff, you know."

"You might as well tell me now."

He sighed. "I know. No, he was just wondering when to pop the question."

"What?!" we both cried.

He chuckled. "The question being if or when to take their chummy relationship onto the next level. They're still just friends, you see, and he's getting a bit frustrated. Only a man can understand that sort of thing."

"Who, you? The Staffordshire Stallion?"

He coloured slightly. "I just told him to take his time. I pointed out that he must have had more... relations than most and if she's special to him he ought to be patient."

"Sound advice," I said.

Linda stood up. "Come on, Sue. Time for our trek."

In our second drawing class we drew cats, dogs and llamas – at Linda's request – before I asked Álvaro for some guidance on landscape drawing. He spoke about the importance of finding a focal point and eliminating unnecessary details, before saying that it would be easier to explain in the open air, as I'd hoped he would.

"We could go out next time if the weather is good," I said.

He smiled stiffly. "I don't go outside much."

"No, and you need to put some colour in... what do you call these?"

"Cheeks."

"You need to put some colour in your cheeks," she said, not an expression used in Spanish, but he understood well enough. We'd deduced that he spent far too much time stuck in his room and had decided to introduce him to the great outdoors.

He'd brought a few small abstract watercolours which to our untrained eyes seemed technically accomplished but rather claustrophobic. One of our New Year's resolutions would be to do our best to widen Álvaro's horizons and maybe help him to meet people other than a middle-aged granny, in my case, and a wannabe granny in Linda's case.

"It's about time he settled down and had kids," she said while we were out drawing from Aunt Jean's ridge on Luke's birthday. She'd called him that morning and his cryptic remarks suggested that he and Sara had partaken of a kiss or two, with more detailed updates to follow on Christmas Day.

"Maybe Sara's the one," I said. "Things seem to have fallen into place for him, don't they?"

"Yes, he's discovered a trade that might suit him and... well, let's not jinx him and the girl. And just think, it's all down to Aunt Jean."

I smiled and surveyed the mountains. "Do you know what I think we should do on Christmas Day?"

"Yes, I think I do."

"Here?"

"Yes, right here."

So it was that the five of us headed for Aunt Jean's ridge on Christmas morning, It was mild and sunny and we took turns at carrying the urn that had adorned our mantelpiece ever since we'd inherited her house. On cresting the rise from the road, Linda led us to our favourite drawing place in the clearing between the pine trees.

"Aunt Jean must have painted on this very spot, so I think we should scatter her ashes here," she said, scuffing the rough ground with her foot.

Bill licked and raised a forefinger. "Hmm, it's a westerly breeze, so if we stand here we'll be sure to cover the place where she once fulfilled her creative urge, time and time again."

Linda and I had debated whether or not to say a prayer, as although Aunt Jean hadn't been a believer when we'd spent time with her, we couldn't be sure she hadn't become more pious later on. In the end, after a little soul searching and a lot of internet research, we'd decided on a poem by Christina Rossetti and had even memorised it, because we thought it so lovely. So, as we all took turns at casting fistfuls of ashes into the breeze, she and I declaimed the following words.

> *"Remember me when I am gone away,*
> *gone far away into the silent land;*
> *When you can no more hold me by the hand,*
> *nor I half turn to go, yet turning stay.*
> *Remember me when no more day by day*
> *you tell me of the future that you planned;*
> *Only remember me; you understand*
> *it will be late to counsel then or pray.*
> *Yet, if you should forget me for a while*
> *and afterwards, remember, do not grieve:*
> *For if the darkness and corruption leave*
> *a vestige of the thoughts that once I had,*
> *better by far you should forget and smile*
> *than that you should remember and be sad."*

"Amen," said Bill solemnly as Linda tipped up the urn and shook it.

"Three cheers for Aunt Jean," said Luke.

"Hip, hip, hooray!" we cried, as there wasn't a soul around.

"I feel guilty again now for not coming to see her," I said, wiping away a tear.

"She never exactly begged you to come," said Paul, ever the pragmatist.

"It would have been nice to have seen her one more time though," said Linda.

"Yes, to thank her for the inheritance," I said.

"I for one shall be eternally grateful," said Luke.

"Me too," said Bill.

"And me," said Paul. "It's chucking it down back home today."

"Who'd have thought last April that we'd all be standing here today?" said Linda.

"And actually living here," I said.

"You know, I think we should visit this spot every Christmas and look back on what we've achieved during the past year," said Bill.

"Yes," said Linda, before peering at her son. "What do you think you'll have achieved by this time next year, Luke?"

He smiled. "Ah, who knows? I have my hopes, but it's too soon to say what'll happen."

"I hope to cycle ten thousand miles for the first time in many years," said Paul.

Linda tutted and shook her head.

"What? It's less than thirty miles a day."

"I may write a book," said Bill.

"What about?" I asked.

"I don't know yet. Something historical, I expect. What about you two?"

Linda snorted. "Sue and I are individuals, Bill."

"I want to improve my Spanish, learn to paint and meet more local people," I said.

"Ditto," said Linda, upon which we all laughed.

Bill patted his stomach. "Time for some turkey, I think."

We set off back to the village.

# THE END

Printed in Great Britain
by Amazon